Pagan and Christian

DEBATES IN ARCHAEOLOGY

Series editor: Richard Hodges

Pagan and Christian

Religious Change in Early Medieval Europe

David Petts

Bristol Classical Press

First published in 2011 by
Bristol Classical Press
an imprint of
Bloomsbury Academic
Bloomsbury Publishing Plc
36 Soho Square,
London W1D 3QY, UK

CIP records for this book are available from the
British Library and the Library of Congress

ISBN 978-0-7156-3754-8

Typeset by Ray Davies
Printed and bound in Great Britain by
CPI Antony Rowe, Chippenham and Eastbourne

www.bloomsburyacademic.com

Contents

To Jane, Isobel and Ned

Acknowledgements

This book has taken far longer to write than originally intended. This has been for domestic and intellectual reasons. The former have included two job changes, two house moves and two children. On the intellectual front, however, it rapidly became clear that inside this slim book lay a huge and sprawling volume trying to escape. Much time was spent on writing text that never made the final cut, although hopefully this will emerge in other forms further down the line. If the writing of this book took a long time, many of the ideas addressed here go back much further. I have been thinking about archaeology and religion ever since I started a PhD on early Christian burial in Britain in the mid-1990s, although the frequent appearance of Martin Carver in this work reflects the profound, if unacknowledged, influence his work had on me as an overenthusiastic undergraduate over twenty years ago.

Over the last fifteen years I have had a chance to explore and exchange thoughts about early medieval Christianity and paganism with numerous colleagues and students. Many may not even be aware that our discussions have helped shape the arguments presented here. They have also been more than helpful in providing practical assistance, particularly in the shape of off-prints and pre-publication copies of new material – inevitably exciting and relevant papers and volumes appear in book catalogues just as one is trying to draw a line under one's writing. In particularly I would like to thank Howard Williams and Sarah Semple in this respect. A special thanks must also go to Deborah Blake of Bristol Classical Press for astounding levels of patience.

1

Early medieval religion in context

Introduction

In 1382 two old enemies died within months of each other. Winrich von Kniprode, Grand Master of the Teutonic Knights, had defeated Kestautis, joint ruler of the Grand Duchy of Lithuania, at the Battle of Rudau twelve years earlier. Enemies in life, their funeral rites speak volumes of the underlying struggle of ideologies that had led to the conflict. Von Kniprode was buried alongside previous masters in the mausoleum that lay beneath the Chapel of St Anna, at the Order's headquarters, the massive red-brick castle of Marienburg (Malbork, Poland). Kestautis, however, was laid out with his horses, weapons, and other belongings and then cremated in the centre of Vilnius, his capital. Von Kniprode was a Christian crusader and Kestautis the ruler of a pagan state; within the year his son Vytautis had converted to Christianity. Their confrontations were the final struggles of the last pagan state in Europe. From now on, the kingdoms of medieval Europe were entirely Christian; only the tiny Emirate of Grenada remained as a lone beacon of non-Christian political power north of the Mediterranean, and its leaders also followed a monotheistic religion that had come to power in the conflict and chaos of late antiquity. The time that had elapsed from the acknowledgement of Christianity as a licit religion by the Roman emperors to the conversion of Vytautis was a little over a thousand years.

In the early fourth century AD Christianity was a minority religion. Although attracting increasing numbers of adherents, it still faced significant persecution, both within the Roman Empire and beyond its borders. It was just one religion in a 'world full of gods' (Hopkins 2000). The religious geography of Europe was complex and shifting, with a mosaic of local religions, national, traditional and international cults. Monotheists, henotheists and polytheists lived and worshipped in close proximity. The relationship between these communities of belief ranged from indifference to open antagonism. Within six hundred years, the religious landscape of Europe was profoundly different; despite undergoing a process of political fission and enduring a deep and fundamental change to the economy and social structures, it was possible to talk about Christendom. Where there was once immense diversity in religion an apparent uniformity of belief could now be seen. Non-Christian religious practice survived only at the margins of society; both at the physical edges of Europe from the animism of the Finno-Ugric peoples of the circumpolar regions to the spread of Islam to the south and east, but also at the social margins of the early medieval world, with small communities of Jews and other communities of alternate belief scattered across Europe (e.g. Berend 2001; Glick 2001). Indeed, the spread of Christianity has come to be seen as one of the features that characterises the medieval world in the first millennium AD. The close link between conversion to the Church and the spread of other key elements of developed medieval society, such as literacy, feudalism and kingship, has often been noted (Bartlett 1993; Berend 2007; Blomkvist 2005). The social impact of Christianity has been amply documented and used as a key tool for exploring the transformation of the post-classical world (Brown 1996; Fletcher 1997; Herrin 1987; Knight 1997); as such the rise of Christendom has become an important meta-narrative for the first millennium AD. Given this, it is not surprising that the study of the Christianisation of European society has become one of the key topics for study by historians and archaeologists working on early medieval material. While the broad chronological contours of the 'spread of the Cross' have been established, there has been a flowering of work developing a more subtle understanding of how this process was played out over time and space (e.g. papers in Carver 2003 and Berend 2007).

1. Early medieval religion in context

This book attempts to take an overview of this renewed interest in 'conversion' and 'Christianisation'. These two phrases will be used again and again the following pages, and the extensive scholarship on religious change in this period has repeatedly attempted to define their precise meaning (e.g. Russell 1994, 26-44; Nock 1933; MacMullen 1984, 1985; Kilbride 2000; Berend 2007, 27-8). While there have been some attempts to move away from this terminology entirely (e.g. Kilbride 2000; Russell 1994), this book will follow the broad consensus among archaeologists and historians of this period and understand 'conversion' as an act in which external allegiance is made to the Church, usually through entering the catechumenate, baptism or 'prime signing', while 'Christianisation' is the longer-term process by which a broadly Christian world view is internalised by individuals and societies. The space between a society seeing its first 'conversions' and its full 'Christianisation' (if such a state is ever achievable) may take decades or even centuries. This book takes as one of its key themes a better understanding of these processes. Rather than trying to provide a chronological or thematic synthesis of the process of conversion (amply covered in a number of recent overviews, e.g. Brown 1996; Fletcher 1997), it is hoped instead to explore some of these methodological and theoretical challenges by working through a number of case studies chosen to shed light on specific issues.

The study of late antique Christianity

One of the key academic divides in the study of early Christianity is that between scholars working on the classical/late antique world and those researching the early medieval world. Few considerations of the spread of the religion attempt to straddle this gulf; while there have been a small number of large-scale narratives that cross this boundary (e.g. Brown 1996; Fletcher 1997), there have been fewer national, regional or local studies that have tackled it. In modern terms, the distinction between late antique and early medieval is a fine

13

one. The dividing line is not chronological; early sixth-century Constantinople would usually be seen as part of the late antique world, while contemporary Yorkshire is seen as firmly early medieval. One of the underlying distinctions is between areas that show some element of direct continuity from classical antiquity and those which seemingly do not (although they may show some evidence of re-using or re-interpreting aspects of the classical past). Not surprisingly the use of such labels can be contentious, as seen clearly in recent debate within British archaeology about how far fifth-century Britain might be seen as late antique rather than early medieval (compare, for example, Esmonde Cleary 2001 with Faulkner 2003).

Inevitably these academic labels also reflect differing emphases in geography and in the range of evidence used. Studies of early Christianity in the classical world have generally focused on the Mediterranean and the Near East (e.g. Macmullen 1984; Hopkins 2000). The approach to the study of Christianity in the classical church has been overwhelmingly text-led, for it is in the lands around the Mediterranean and the Persian Gulf that the writers behind these texts dwelt. In contrast to these synthetic overviews, the studies of the spread of Christianity in the provinces during the Roman period have often been far more archaeological in context, reflecting the relative lack of textual material (e.g. Gaspar 2002; Knight 1999; Migotti 1997; Petts 2003).

While the study of patristics, the documentary output of the early church fathers, forms a key plank in the textual study of late antique conversion, it is not the only one. This was also a world of erudite and persuasive pagan intellectuals. This has allowed scholars to explore the process of Christianisation as the creation of a discourse not just within the community of Christian writers, but between Christianity and classical paganism. To a certain extent both sides of the theological debate can be explored through the voices and writings of the key participants. Nonetheless these pagan voices are drawn from a relatively limited section of the wider pagan community. By definition, these writers are literate and almost without exception drawn from an educated élite. The form of paganism which these writers was a relatively limited and circumscribed form of non-Christian belief which includes strongly orphic and Gnostic tendencies and theologies closely linked to ideas formulated in the Platonic philosophical tradition (Chuvin 1990). These types of paganism are clearly just a small and relatively arcane element of the far wider cluster of pagan practices that could be found across the Empire; their literary evidence may allow us to view a pagan-Christian dialogue, but it was a limited and rarefied one.

The sheer quantity of textual material available has had a profound impact on the way in which late antique Christianity has been explored. It would not be unfair to argue that the focus on patristics has meant that for long the underlying meta-narrative has emphasised the development of theology and dogma. Religious change was not necessarily however simply a consequence of the successful defence of an intellectual standpoint. As with any paradigm shift, whether at a personal or institutional level, this transition was effected as much through the demands of *realpolitik*, the pragmatics of power that run through all aspects of society and the social and material constraints of daily life. As will be explored elsewhere in this book, the problematic relationship between religious belief and religious practice is one that permeated debates about religions in past societies, and continues to exist as a key problematic in modern studies of the history of religion (McCarthy 2009). However, the emphasis on text-led investigations of religious change in the classical world has a tendency to privilege the study of belief over practice.

The work of Peter Brown from the 1960s and 1970s in exploring the wider socio-cultural impact of Christianity was of fundamental importance in moving the study of religious change and the creation of the Christian world out of the scriptorium and into the rough and tumble of the late antique world. For example, Brown's *The Body and Society* (1988), which clearly demonstrated the influence of Michel Foucault, explored the impact of Christianity on the body through its examination of the relationship between sexuality and power in the late antique world. This stimulated a substantial body of consequent research (e.g. Shaw 1998; Schroeder 2007; Cox Miller 2009) which takes the body as point of departure to explore early Christianity. However, ironically these explorations of the body remain curiously disembodied, focusing primarily on texts and high-status art as the principal types of evidence used. There is little real engagement with materiality of the body as expressed through the physical artefacts which they used and adorned themselves and the built spaces through which they moved, forms of evidence that archaeology might be best suited to explore. For a long time the study of late antique and early Christian art had been dominated by connoisseurship and a traditional art history (e.g. Grabar 1967; Van der Meer 1967). The 'material turn' in the study of late antiquity initiated by Brown certainly stimulated an increased interest in the potential for the study of art in exploring rather than simply illustrating the process of Christianisation (e.g Elsner 1995; McCormick 1981). However, these studies have drawn primarily on élite, luxury and public art rather than on more mundane objects and artefacts. The one area where the study of conversion has clearly intersected with the wider social environment has been the exploration of the way in which the impact of the adoption of Christianity by the Roman state transformed the urban landscape of the classical world (e.g. Harries 1992; Wharton 1995; Loseby and Christie 1996).

As a result of these tendencies within the study of religion, the study of Christian conversion has been dominated by an approach that might be characterised as focusing on the development of a discourse between Christian and a limited pagan audience carried out primarily through texts and high-status art. A significant proportion of the Christian and pagan participants in this discourse in fact shared key cultural reference points despite their apparent religious differences. This shared cultural knowledge, which included grounding in classical mythology, Platonic philosophy, rhetoric, grammar and oratory transcended the more obvious religious disagreements of many writers (Brown 1992). An appreciation of this common élite intellectual culture is essential; it was deliberately cultivated and may have provided a unifying sense of identity and cultural reference points that allowed any dialogue between Christian and pagan at all. However, this common repertoire of knowledge also highlight the limitations of exploring the articulation of Christian and pagan world views, whether found in the textual corpus or the high-status products of Mediterranean *ateliers*, as they are both drawing on a common stock of literary and artistic tropes. It is a methodological challenge for the modern scholar to break out of the confines of this discourse; something which an archaeological approach to the study of religious practice allows.

The study of early medieval Christianity

These distinctive features of the study of religious change and conversion in the late classical world contrast with the approaches used to explore similar concerns by scholars working on 'early medieval' regions. As with the study of late antiquity, the 'early medieval' world has distinct geographical limits and is generally regarded as including those areas of the Roman Empire that underwent a period of apparent rupture due to a greater or lesser extent of Barbarian immigration. These include most of England and much of western, southern and south-eastern Europe, particularly beyond the Danube. The early medieval world also comprises those areas of northern Europe that were never integrated into the Roman Empire; essentially a crescent running from Ireland through Scotland across the North Sea to Scandinavia, Eastern Germany and the Baltic. These areas have more in common than simply geography or immediate history. While it is always a risk to generalise, the polities in these areas generally tended to be small-scale political formations constructed around personalised power relations with socially embedded, and generally localised, economies. Urbanism and coinage was almost completely absent until the eighth century AD at earliest, when their appearance appears to have gone hand-in-hand with the extension and consolidation of long-distance trade networks. These were also, generally speaking, non-literate societies, though not entirely so, as will be explored below. This is in contrast to the urbanised and literate societies with monetised economies and state bureaucracies that characterised much of the late antique world.

These differences also extend to the approaches taken to the process of religious conversion – it is a critical exploration of these approaches that will form the heart of this book. The first key difference is the extent of surviving textual evidence. However one measures it, the total resource is far less than in the Mediterranean world. There are also significant areas, particularly much of Scandinavia and the Baltic, where contemporary documentary records are almost entirely absent. In some cases, these absences genuinely reflect the lack of textual production in these areas; in other cases, such as Wales and Pictish Scotland, this absence probably reflects the failure of early texts to survive for a host of reasons (Sims-Williams 1998, 18-24; Forsyth 1998, 39-44). Unlike the late antique world, the surviving textual material is entirely a product of a Christian cultural milieu; there is no pagan Bede or Henry of Livonia engaging in written dialogue with Christian scholars or producing counter-narratives with which to contest the totalising discourse of the Christian literati.

Further challenges presented by the textual material are linked to one of the key differences in the process of religious change within the rump of the Roman Empire and outside it. With the Edict of Milan in AD 313 the Christian church was able to assume a position of first-among-equals and became the *de facto* state religion in the Empire; the existing cells of Christianity were able to break cover and rapidly became integrated with many of the existing power structures within the Roman state. Christian writers such as Eusebius soon developed an ideological accommodation between the Church and the state that saw a close elision between religious (Christian) and political (Roman) identity (Fletcher 1997, 28-30). Almost by definition there was no drive to extend the geographic boundary of Christendom beyond the physical limits of the Empire in the fourth century AD. Whatever the processes that led to the conversion of the bulk of the population, the primary motors for change emerged from within society.

In contrast, in the early medieval world, the initial drivers and religious change were almost always external and were equipped with a much more explicitly worked out theology of mission which demanded that the pagans be converted. In some cases, such as in the Anglo-Saxon world, these external stimuli for religious change took the form of missionaries, sent either by Rome (such as Gregory the Great's commission of Augustine to convert Anglo-Saxon England) or other power centres (such as the missionary work by Anskar or Boniface promoted by the Carolingian court) to encourage conversion through persuasion and political intrigue. In other cases, particularly in the Baltic, the catalyst for religious change took a far more physical and coercive turn, through the presence of bodies of aggressive and heavily armed knights (Christiansen 1997; Eihmane 2009).

Whatever form this initial push towards religious change took, and however the subsequent practical extension of Christian belief may have taken shape, the idea that Christianity is something that is introduced from outside is a key notion that pervades medieval hagiography and historical writing. In this sense, the spread of Christianity might be interpreted as an essentially colonial project; with the promotion and extension of Christendom in practice leading to the extension of existing networks of secular and ecclesiastical power into new areas. Thus it is possible to identify two classes of early textual material dealing with religious change; narratives which record the physical extension and consolidation of Christianity (such as Bede's *Ecclesiastical History*, Alcuin's *Vita Willibrordi* or Rimbert's *Vita Ansgarii*) and narrative and other material (such as penitentials and chronicles) that record the consolidation and accommodation of Christianity within existing societies. Examples of the latter might include the late eighth-

19

century Carolingian *Capitulatio de Partibus Saxoniae,* Martin of Braga's *De Correctione Rusticorum*, or the later ninth-century *Replies of Pope Nicholas to the Questions of the Bulgars* (Effros 1997; Sullivan 1966) The latter appear in both late antique and early medieval contexts, but the former are mainly limited to the early medieval world of Northern and Eastern Europe. It can be seen that the range of textual evidence for the development of Christianity in these areas is different from the suite of evidence available to the scholar of the late antique Mediterranean. While they lack the texts produced by pagans in opposition and debate with Christianity, they instead have access to different genres of literary output, the missionary narrative.

As well as differences in the nature of the literary evidence derived from early medieval contexts, the role of archaeology in the study of conversion takes a far more central place. This is doubtless due to the relative lack of textual material compared with the late antique world. There are however some distinct aspects of the archaeological record that attract more interest than others. The study of the impact of conversion on mortuary behaviour and burial rituals is one which attracts particular focus. We can see burial archaeology and the study of Christianisation coming together in two related ways. The first is the use of key, high-status, and usually unique, burials as a lens to explore the impact of religious change; for example, the sumptuous burial found beneath Mound 1 at Sutton Hoo (Suffolk) (Carver 2005) has become a key site through which the conversion of Anglo-Saxon England is explored, being seen variously as a the burial of an early convert or an avowedly pagan response to the new religion. The funerary complex at Jelling (Denmark) is linked to the conversion of Denmark by Harold Bluetooth in the tenth century AD and has become a site through which contesting interpretations of the nature of conversion can be debated (e.g. Staecker 2005). Other such focal sites include the grave of Childeric at Tournai (Halsall 2001) and Gamla Uppsala (Nordahl 1996). Crucially, all these graves are the burials of key individuals who can with greater or

1. Early medieval religion in context

lesser certainty be linked to identifiable figures from historic narratives, allowing archaeological explorations to be keyed in to chronologies supplied by written texts.

A second area in which early medieval archaeology has engaged with the study of Christianisation has been the obsession with recognising Christianity in the burial rite. The study of burial has been one of the dominant methodological foci of early medieval archaeologists. Burial rites of much of early medieval Europe included consistent deposition of grave-goods, particularly personal dress items. The highly visible burials contrast with the more ephemeral nature of settlement archaeology. Burial archaeology is thus crucial for methodological reasons; the graves contain sealed contexts containing material culture that can be dated through typological analysis. Variations in the type and position of objects in the grave can be seen not only as a consequence of chronological change, but also as guided by the creation and maintenance of certain forms of social identity, such as gender and ethnicity. However, the practice appears to have died out across most of Europe over the latter half of the first millennium AD (e.g. Geake 1997). This phenomenon appears to very broadly coincide with the spread of Christianity, which has been seen as being a key causative factor; the absence of grave-goods being seen as a clear indicator of Christian identity (e.g. Meaney and Hawkes 1970, 53; Graslund 1981, 84; Wessman 2010, 80).

Other key features linked to the rise of a distinctive Christian mortuary rite include the move towards a consistent west-east orientation and the cessation of burial in previously 'pagan' cemeteries (e.g. Hyslop 1963, 190-1; Meaney and Hawkes 1970, 51-2; Thomas 1981, 228-39). This whole notion was predicated on the seemingly not unreasonable assumption that as burial was a religious rite, a change in religion should lead to a change in burial practice. Despite some important critical engagement with the methodological problems associated with this simplistic model (e.g. Bullough 1983; Hadley 2000), the critique of the essentialist model of a Christian burial rite has often been relatively unsophisticated. The most

21

common critical response has been to highlight 'spoilers': usually examples of the burials of individuals of known Christian affiliation, such as Childeric or Cuthbert, who were inhumed with grave-goods. While this obviously gives the lie to a simplistic equation between absence of grave-goods and Christianity, it runs the risk of denying any relationship at all between Christianity and mortuary rituals.

While the use of burial in explicating the conversion process brings archaeological material into focus, there are still tensions in the relationship between historical and archaeological approaches to the topic. A good example of this can be seen in one of the key metanarratives that underlie many histories of early medieval religious change, the so-called 'Constantinian' model of conversion. This model has its origins in Constantine's adoption of Christianity in 312; the version of these events promoted by Eusebius acted as an influential model for later conversion narratives and strategies well into the post-medieval period (e.g. Provost-Smith 2009). The underlying metanarrative argues that conversion was driven by monarchs who chose to convert for solid political reasons in order to ally themselves with other powerful individuals, usually for short-term political gain. In some cases the rulers act entirely at their own volition and in circumstances of their own choosing, in other cases, there is external encouragement (Berend 2007; Mayr-Harting 1991; Sanmark 2004; Yorke 2003). Following initial conversion by the king, the more drawn-out process of Christianisation is then seen as trickling down through the ranks of society through the medium of missionaries, reaching the poorest and most marginalised last of all. While in some cases there may have been an element of consultation (e.g. Clovis: Gregory of Tours II.29-31 or Edwin: *HE* I.25-6, II.9-14) the ultimate decision to convert is the king's. It is rare to find occasions when a conversion narrative shows a ruler as genuinely seeming to defer to wider popular political considerations and sensibilities, such as Olof's extensive equivocation in the light of Anskar's second visit to Birka (*Vita Ansgarii* 27).

This process of hegemonic conversion represents the spread

of the religion as being essentially contingent on the ebbs and flows of early medieval micro- and macro-politics. A more developed version of this argument suggests that conversion was undertaken for short-term gain, but also to enable rulers to access a range of 'resources', primarily ideological (e.g. models of kingship), but also practical (e.g. literacy), which would allow them to consolidate their rule (Brown 1996, 340-54; Higham 1997; Kloczowski 1993; Urbanczyk 2003). It is certainly true that in an early medieval political landscape the central role of a king in matters of belief would have been of fundamental importance. Kings would be able to facilitate or prevent missionary activity, and would be in a position to materially reward those who converted and punish those who did not. They were also able to deploy significant material resources, particularly land, but also movable wealth (including slaves) which would allow the Church to consolidate its position within a given society. There have been more recent critiques which have argued that kings were not entirely free agents and that they were reliant on networks of local alliances and power relationships within their kingdoms, including their families and non-royal élites, and as such were not entirely free agents (e.g. Tyler 2007). However, even these critiques still see the decision to convert by a monarch as essentially an exercise in *realpolitik* exercised within a range of constraints. Nonetheless, the focus in this narrative is the 'sender' rather than the 'receiver' (Andersson 2000, 134). For the bulk of the population the conversion process is largely untheorised, being assumed to have occurred through a largely unexplained 'trickle-down effect' (Fletcher 1997, 236).

This narrative is primarily one that was developed by historians rather than archaeologists. This is not surprising; the majority of conversion narratives were created within the context of direct or indirect royal patronage; Bede's alignment with the ruling house of Northumbria is a classic example of this kind of relationship. Significantly, Bede's *Ecclesiastical History* was an important model for others writing conversion narratives in early medieval Europe, such as the narrative of

Hungarian conversion written by Pilgrim, Bishop of Passau (971-991 AD) (Berend, Laszlovsky and Szakács 2007, 329-30). More general perpetuations of the Constantinian model can be seen in a range of other written sources, such as Thietmar of Merseburg's *Chronicon* which presented the people of Poland as one body with Miezko I (who initiated conversion in Poland) as its head (Urbanczyk and Rosik 2007; *Chronicon* IV.56); the primacy of Miezko in initiating Christianisation has been consolidated by the lack of alternative historical narratives (Urbanczyk and Rosik 2007, 275). In some cases the parallel with Constantine was made explicit: the *Russian Primary Chronicle* described Vladimir the Great, instigator of conversion among the Kievan Rus, as 'the new Constantine of mighty Rome, who baptised himself and also his subjects' (*RPC* 124-6). Not surprisingly these narratives emphasised the key role of monarchs in conversion. While modern scholarship may have subjected the narratives to close readings allowing alternative motivations for the individual royal decisions to be proposed, they are still only able to explore the process through the limited cast of kings and nobles supplied by the medieval chroniclers. Any story of early medieval conversion based on such documentary sources can only be one of top-down religious change; the evidence does not easily allow us to write any others.

This narrative of Christian conversion as seen from an élite perspective has been profoundly influential among archaeologists. This is seen most clearly in a focus on monumentality. Early medieval archaeology took this 'monumental turn' in the 1990s, drawing particularly on the work of prehistorians such as Richard Bradley and John Barrett (e.g. Barrett 1990; Bradley 1987; 1998a; Williams 2006: 145-79). The creation of monuments, understood in the widest sense of the word, including stone crosses, churches, monasteries and cathedrals, is a process that almost by definition requires significant investment in time and real and social capital. Whether mobilising dozens of members of a kinship group to construct a boat grave, investing in the wide range of exotic materials required to make an illuminated gospel book or contracting in foreign masons to build a church, monumentality in the early medieval period is almost invariably a socio-political strategy that can be deployed only by wealthy individuals or corporate groups. This is not to suggest that investment in monumental structures does not occur in more egalitarian societies, but simply to recognise that early medieval societies were ranked and had differential access to resources depending on status. As such, monuments were 'fields of discourse' where social dynamics could be played out and enacted, but within defined physical and social parameters. Inevitably, the focus on monumentality in archaeological discussions of conversion and Christianisation is also a consequence of the nature of the archaeological record; Christianised rune stones, stone sculptural traditions and cathedral complexes leave very clear impressions in the archaeological record and often contain explicit references to a Christian ideology, such as the use of crosses and other distinctively religious symbolism. This high visibility often contrasts with other aspects of the early medieval archaeological record, such as settlement sites, which can be more elusive in the field. A focus on monumentality in understanding early medieval conversion is particularly visible in the work of Martin Carver and a series of scholars emerging from the University of York, who have plotted the spread and development of Christianity in Britain and beyond through a discourse of monument construction and use (Carver 2001; 2002; Dobson 2008; Toop 2005).

This tradition of focussing on monumentality in the conversion period should not be lightly dismissed. As with élite-focussed historical narratives, it engages with the most conspicuous aspects of the evidential base, and whether we are looking at archaeological or historical approaches, they are both primarily tackling a resource, textual and monumental, produced by a powerful group of social actors. Equally, the fact that these documents and structures are the most visible expressions of Christianity in early medieval society is not simply a quirk of the subsequent 'taphonomy' of the evidential base;

the high visibility of this material is an important issue, and as noted above, the élites undoubtedly were profoundly and closely implicated in the spread of Christianity in this period. I would argue not that this approach is wrong, but that it is limited. The focus on the spectacular and the highly visible means that other potential indices of religious change, such as changes in diet, dress or even refuse disposal, are not interrogated. There is a danger of perpetuating the notion that conversion is something is recognisable only at élite level, and that variation or variety in the evidence is primarily the consequence of variation in specific socio-political strategies mobilised and materialised by key social actors within early medieval society. This clearly runs the risk of seeing the mechanisms of conversion as contingent upon political events and the inter-relationships of élite power structures, with an associated lack of agency being attributed to both the drivers of conversion, particularly missionaries, and those who chose to convert (Kilbride 2000, 12-14). Religion is seen as ultimately an aspect of politics that achieved success as a result of its functional ability to help structure and finesse the new articulations of power linked to the spread of kingship in the first millennium AD. This ignores other motives for conversion, including genuine belief, ontological insecurity or even agendas of political resistance and non-conformity.

The danger in developing a reductionist narrative that limits the spread of Christianity to political imperatives is the failure to tackle variety in Christian practice that is recognisable in the archaeological and historical record. Early Christianity was undoubtedly heterodox; Arianism, Pelagianism and Monophysitism were clearly significant strands of belief in the religious landscape of late antiquity; however, these were more or less successfully repressed, particularly in the West, and there was, in theory at least, a uniformity of belief. Nonetheless, there is clear evidence for regional variety in the expression of Christianity across early medieval Europe, belying the notional theological unity expressed through the Nicene Creed (Pluskowski and Patrick 2003). This can be recognised in burial practice, church architecture, the development of relic cults, the spatial organisation of ecclesiastical sites, monastic tonsures and a multiplicity of other elements of religious life. Importantly, this variety was in practice and institutional organisation rather than in doctrine; recognition of heteropraxy in the historical or archaeological record need not be predicated on the presence of heterodoxy within the Church. There have been wider attempts to deconstruct notions of a monolithic early medieval church (e.g. Pluskowski and Patrick 2003; Kilbride 2000). These have particular questioned the 'essentialist' model of Christianity (and paganism), highlighting the sheer diversity in practice found across European Christendom, both at a gross level, such as the tension between the Roman Latin and Byzantine Greek traditions, but also at micro-level. They also emphasise the dynamic nature of belief. Christian practice could change over time, and the notion that there was ever an 'essential' model for Christianity that held true across time and space is ultimately misguided (see Chapter 2 for a more detailed critique of essentialist models of belief).

There has always been some recognition of variation within the western church, with a long tradition of identifying distinctive 'ethnic' churches, such as the 'Celtic church' or the 'Frankish church' (Davies 1992; Wallace-Hadrill 1983) and the German historiographical construct of *gentilkirchen,* churches that 'derived their cohesion from a polity with a shared ethnic identity' (De Jong 2006, 117). Rather than simply identifying national church traditions, there has been a move towards to developing a more nuanced understanding of the variation in Christianity in this period. Peter Brown introduced the concept of 'micro-christendoms' reflecting this variation in religious activity in Europe: small-scale and regionally distinctive churches that saw themselves as 'reflecting in microcosm, in their own land, the imagined, all embracing macrocosm of a world-wide Christianity' (Brown 1996, 218). Carver has also been keen to demonstrate how the way in which early Christianity developed institutionally could vary; for example, some areas developed on simple episcopal lines, others saw the more extensive spread of monasticism, while further areas saw the establishment of a 'secular' church dominated by proprietary churches (*eigenkirchen; eigenkloster*) (e.g. Carver 1998a, 2001). More recently he has explored how monumentality can be used to delineate 'intellectual communities' at a regional and sub-regional level in Anglo-Saxon England, with areas having different modes of monumentality (Carver 2010). Importantly, he has argued that these communities cannot be easily mapped onto the known political geography of the English kingdoms, and that we are instead seeing the physical expression of otherwise submerged ideological or intellectual programmes that are not apparent through the documentary record. In this, his 'intellectual communities' are subtly different from Brown's micro-christendoms which can be more directly mapped onto the political organisations of this period. Different modes of institutional expression can be found in differing areas of the same kingdom. Indeed the fluid and pullulating polities of the early medieval world are often notably less stable than some elements of the religious infrastructure, and Carver has suggested that these variations in religious practice may have their origins in long-lasting *mentalités* that transcend the *conjonctures* of political events (Carver 2009).

These models are useful as ways of understanding variety in religious experience in first-millennium Europe. However, they do have some limitations. Despite implicit attempts to move away from the essentialist models of early medieval Christianity, they still, in some ways, perpetuate some aspects of this notion. The key challenge they do not confront is the range of dimensions in which variety of religious practice can be recognised. In both cases, the emphasis is on mapping variety spatially. While Brown's micro-christendoms are more closely tied to the spatial extent of medieval polities than Carver's 'intellectual communities', they both fail to engage adequately with the extent to which engagement with Christianity, and early religion in general, can vary within a given social unit. They do not engage with the alternative ways in which Christianity might have been experienced by, for example, women, unfree members of the society, ethnic minorities and, importantly, those who chose not convert. Even potentially discordant voices from within the élite itself risk being ignored if religious variety is mapped only spatially. This inherent focus on the religious experience of the politically powerful is to the detriment of the voices of the more socially marginalised members of society (who may, in terms of numbers, be the majority). Christianisation is again seen as something that happens via the aristocracy. It is only with these élite groups that any element of agency in the process of religious change is vested; the rest of the population simply passively respond to the power-struggles of an aristocratic minority.

It is here that we reach the limits of the dominant model of 'hegemonic conversion'; whether looking at the documents produced by churchmen or the monumental investment of the nobility, the narrative is limited to one in which a dominant ideology is imposed and perpetuated by the upper echelons of society. There is no room for alternative narratives or discourses from below that critique or contest this version of events. It is in attempting to re-address this balance that archaeology comes into its own in the study of early medieval religion. While the archaeological record might be dominated by the monumental, whether burial mounds or churches, it also contains the evidence for far more than the relics of large-scale investment by the élites. By changing the scale of analysis it should be possible to identify the expression of belief at a wider range of resolutions than simply the spectacular.

2

Approaching religion: archaeology and belief

Anthropological studies of religious change have often examined the transition from what are characterised as small-scale, local or tribal religions to large-scale, universal, world religions (including Christianity, Islam, Judaism, Hinduism, etc.) (Bowie 2000, 26; Hefner 1993b; Mensching 1964; Morris 1990, 68-9). This distinction ultimately appears to have its origins in the works of key scholars such as Max Weber, who distinguished between 'world' and 'primitive' religions (Weber 1956). Out of this dichotomy has sprung a series of stereotyped images of these two types of religion which I would suggest has influenced the way in which they are studied.

LOCAL RELIGION versus	WORLD RELIGION
diverse	uniform
local	international
small-scale	large-scale
microcosm	macrocosm
inchoate	structured
creative	prescribed
ritual	religion
heterodox	orthodox
superstitious	rational
cyclical time	linear time (eschatology/ teleology)
performance	liturgy
world accepting	world rejecting
inclusive	exclusive
sensual	ascetic
libidinous	moral
timeless	historical
ethnic	universal
PAGAN	CHRISTIAN
archaeology/anthropology?	history?

2. Approaching religion: archaeology and belief

This simple binary opposition of local/world religions has often been used by historians and archaeologists to explore processes of religious change (e.g. Russell 1994; Urbanczyk 2003), although this clearly simplistic model is being increasingly critiqued by scholars working on early medieval topics (e.g. Higham 1997; Kilbride 2000, 8). It is important to be aware of the intellectual and historiographical context of such superficially seductive models of religion. Such categories were developed by both anthropologists drawing directly on ethnographic fieldwork, and sociologists and historians of religions drawing on primary anthropological research (Morris 1990). However, such work, particularly in the nineteenth and early twentieth centuries, was carried out in within the institutional context of both European and US colonialism and significant missionary activity, with much important ethnographic work being undertaken by Christian missionaries (Asad 1973; Shaw 1990; Pels 1997, 172; Sanneh 1989). Heavily influenced by Judaeo-Christian notions of what defined 'religion', missionaries attempted to translate indigenous religious practices into terms that could be either assimilated or rejected by the church, according to their similarity to Christianity. This reflects a wider impetus towards 'categorisation' as part of the colonial project (e.g. Said 1994; Cohn 1996), a process which saw indigenous cultures reinterpreted in terms that could be more easily understood by colonial rulers and administrators, and these interpretations then used to facilitate the articulation of social, political and cultural power (Pels 1997). The construction of dualist models was common within such contexts; as Rosalind Shaw notes: 'the "world religions"/ "traditional religions" distinction is in a direct line of descent from the evolutionary theories of the nineteenth century ethnologists, via the dualistic comparisons of "primitive" and "modern" modes of thought by early twentieth century anthropological theorists' (Shaw 1990, 342). Ultimately, local religions are defined in opposition to privileged 'world religions'; they become everything that world religions are not, rather than being explored as a subject in their own right.

31

While the use of such sequences of binary oppositions is common within some areas of archaeology, particularly those influenced by (post-)structuralism (e.g. Tilley 1994, 20-1; Hodder and Hutson 2005, 45-52), in practice they suggest a spurious consistency and rigidity in the simplistic categorisations from which they derive. Critiques of such models have noted that in practice such approaches to categorisation are difficult to impose consistently. For example, Judaism, usually categorised as a 'world religion', is generally restricted to a specific ethnic group (a feature more usually associated with 'local religions'), while some small-scale or localised cults may be open to converts (Shaw 1990). Equally importantly, many religions include aspects of both categories; Christianity includes a clear sense of linear time, but incorporates a strong element of cyclical time in its celebration of the liturgical year (see Chapter 4). At best, such simple categorisations may offer a series of individual axes of analysis with particular expressions of religion being situated variably along a spectrum rather than polarised at one extreme or another. Nonetheless, this construction of 'world' v. 'local' religions, whether acknowledged explicitly or assumed implicitly, has important implications for an understanding of how patterns of religious change in the early medieval world have been characterised by previous scholars.

The first challenge is the easy slide from the categorisation of religions to the construction of an evolutionary typology. While the simple binary model for religions should not in theory imply any sense of chronological progression, it is often used that way. The notion of a series of evolutionary stages in the development of religions is an old one and can be found in the work of such key figures as Durkheim and Tylor (Durkheim 1976; Tylor 1958), with such typologies invariably moving from animism through polytheism and culminating with monotheistic world religions at the pinnacle of religious evolution. These evolutionary approaches to religion were just one aspect of the wider development of social evolutionary approaches to past societies with all the teleological implications that come with them. It is not surprising that models of religious and societal progression were closely interlinked with the development of monotheism being closely tied to the development of the proto-state (see Chapter 1).

There is also a clear sense of value judgement inherent in such typologies. When used in a colonial or ethnographic context, the clear convergence of *world religion*, colonialism and modernity is particularly problematic. As well as implying that 'world religions' have higher social or political value, evolutionary approaches also inherently imply that they have a greater functional value than 'local religions'. This can be seen expressed most clearly in the close link regularly ascribed between conversion and early medieval state formation, explored in Chapter 1, with the advent of Christianity being better fitted to the creation of a centralised polities than paganism, which is seen as inherently particularist and atomistic.

A second challenge presented by these simple binary models of religion is the danger of a fundamentally essentialist conception of Christianity and paganism. Such essentialist models of Christianity result in the representation of a system of religious belief that shows no variation in time or across space. This ultimately results in Christianity and paganism becoming decontextualised units of analysis divorced from temporal or spatial contingencies (Kilbride 2000). For the archaeologist this manifests itself in adoption of a simple relationship between a religion and its material correlates and finds its extremes in the creation of checklists of what a Christian burial or a church *ought* to look like (e.g. Watts 1991, 38-98; for a further critique see Cookson 1987). Scholars often assume a uniformity in practice and belief that simply did not exist. The challenge presented by the seductive lure of essentialist approaches to religion has been increasingly recognised as presenting a fundamental conceptual challenge for scholars studying early Christianity (e.g. Kilbride 2000; Pluskowski and Patrick 2003). However, essentialist models present equal challenges for those wishing to explore the murky world of early medieval paganism; this will be explored in more detail in Chapter 4.

The irony, of course, is that attempts by modern scholars to construct a uniform model of early Christianity mirror the struggle by the early church to impose both orthodoxy (consistency of belief) and orthopraxy (consistency of practice) on its followers. While uniformity may have been an ideal yearned for by the early church, the struggle against heresy and the continued attempts to condense the fundamentals of Christianity into a simple creed simply highlight the fissile tendencies found within even the most structured religion (Cameron 1993, 21-5, 64-7). For example, one of the most important debates was predicated on something as simple as a difference as one letter: *homoousion* (of the Nicene Creed) or *homoiousion* (of the semi-Arians). It is important, however, to realise how often these struggles could be fought out over material aspects of religion. Even in the earliest years of the church the struggle between the Petrine and Pauline factions could be focussed on a physical sign; the presence or absence of the foreskin (Gal. 2, 3; Gal. 5, 2). Equally the iconoclasm of sixth-century Byzantium hinged on the relationship between material objects and God (Kitzinger 1954; Cameron 1979). Yet again the variation in tonsure between the northern church of Colman and the Roman church of Wilfrid was capable of crystallising the differences between the two factions as clearly as the difference in celebrating Easter (Mayr-Harting 1991, 230).

We are of course led to a challenging problem. If we reject an essentialist model of Christianity, whether presented as checklists for use by archaeologists or the use of the Nicene creed as a 'benchmark' of orthodoxy by the dominant early medieval European manifestation of the church, then how do we define Christianity? The alternative is a more avowedly relativistic approach; Christianity is what people who say they are Christians do. Such relativistic approaches have been criticised for making comparisons between Christian and pagan religious practices difficult (Russell 1994, 35; cf. Kilbride 2000). However, rather than seeing subjective and 'emic' definitions as being problematic, we should instead acknowledge the potential of such approaches. It is in the very tensions between belief and practice, the doctrine of Nicene Creed and the practices of the 'micro-Christendoms' that we can start exploring what it meant to be Christian in the first millennium AD and address the different ways in which Christian belief could be enacted. If relativist, or at least constructivist, perceptions complicate comparisons between belief systems, this is something that should be acknowledged, indeed celebrated. It is in the messy detail of religious practice rather than in doctrinal exegesis that we can best understand the lived experience of early medieval religion.

An identity approach to the study of religion

In the move towards relativism and away from essentialist definitions, the debates centring around early medieval conversion can be seen to parallel another one of the key topics within the field of early medieval studies, the creation and maintenance of ethnic identities.

Much recent scholarship has focused on the process of ethnogenesis in early medieval Europe, exploring and problematising ethnic identity (e.g. papers in Pohl and Reimitz 1998; Halsall 2007, 35-62). These debates have moved our models of ethnicity from nineteenth- and early twentieth-century conceptions of ethnic groups which saw a convergence of cultural identity, biological descent and language use, an approach that has its origins in European historical and archaeological traditions of culture history. Instead contemporary approaches to early medieval ethnicity emphasise the fluid and contextually specific expression of identity found in the historic and archaeological record (e.g. Geary 1983; Curta 2005). This reflects wider works on identity and archaeology which can be characterised by a number of key propositions (see Jones 1997, 106-27):

35

1. Ethnic identities are not given; they are created, they are a product of society.
2. Ethnic identities are contested. Identities are the focus for debate and often rely for their existence on tension with other identities.
3. Identities are multi-layered. One individual may have many different identities.
4. These identities are context-specific. Individuals may consider themselves in different ways, depending upon their position,
5. Identity is political. It may be used as a tool for repression and resistance. It is not a neutral label.

Accepting these propositions, it is possible to see conversion as an infinitely complex process. Christianity is just one new identity out of many identities available for individuals in the early middle ages. The extent and the manner in which Christianity operates within a society reflects the way in which religion is used as a marker of social identity. As well as offering a new overarching identity as a member of the Christian faith, it also offers a series of clustered identities: such as membership of a diocese, devotion to a particular saint, or affiliation to an ecclesiastical community. These complement pre-existing identities such as kinship, tribe, gender, age or status. The political use of a Christian identity has already been mentioned, and the creation of local senses of identity as a way of social control has also been hinted at. There is ultimately no authentic way of expressing Christianity, but merely a suite of different strategies appropriate for different contexts. If ethnicity is a situational construct then so is religious practice.

This has implications for the way in which archaeologists study Christianity. Material culture is not a simple reflection of religious affiliation. In the same way that it may actively help to create ethnic identity, material culture may actively help to formulate what it is to be Christian. Variations in material culture should be seen as reflecting the varying ways in which

Christianity is used. Importantly, the expression of religious identity was contextually specific. The way people express their religion can vary temporally and spatially (Barker 1993, 204-6). Models of conversion must be 'multi-causal rather than mono-causal' (Ikenga-Metuh 1987, 11-27). Rather than limiting our explanations to only ontological changes or institutional changes, or the niceties of dynastic politics or the complex waters of shifting social identities we need to consider all aspects of religious change.

The challenge for those researching early medieval religion is to identify the sites and moments in which religious identities are expressed. Rather than assuming that these will be consistent over time and space or even between pagan and Christian practice, it is the variation in the contexts in which religious identity and belief is enacted that becomes of one of the key fields of study. This can be better understood through a broad consideration of the religious content of early medieval burial practice. We have already seen that mortuary rites have long been one of the key areas in which religious changes have been explored (see Chapter 1). Ultimately this approach is underpinned by the basic assumption that in all societies burial is fundamentally a religious act. However, there is good evidence to suggest that the early church was relatively unconcerned about the religious dimension of burial. This can perhaps be seen most clearly in Sulpicius Severus' *Life of St Martin of Tours* (12:1-5):

> It happened during the following period that while he was on a journey he came across the corpse of a pagan which was being carried out for burial in accordance with superstitious funeral rites. Seeing in the distance a crowd of people coming towards him, he stopped awhile, not knowing what it was. For he was about 500 paces away so it was difficult to make out what he was seeing. However, because he could see a group of peasants and the linen cloths laid over the corpse fluttering in the wind he thought they were performing pagan sacrificial rites for it

was the custom of the peasants in Gaul in their pitiable delusion to carry demonic representations, covered with a white veil, over their fields. And so Martin raised his hand and made the sign of the cross against those who were coming towards him. He ordered the crowd to stop and to set down what they were carrying. And now you would have seen an amazing thing. These miserable people first became rigid like rocks; then, when they made a great effort to move forward they found that they were unable to move any further and went spinning round in a ridiculous whirling movement until they were overcome with dizziness and set down the burden of the corpse. They looked round at each other in amazement, wondering in silence at what had happened. But when the holy man understood that *these people had gathered for a funeral, not a religious ceremony* [my emphasis], he raised his hand once more and granted them the power to depart and carry the corpse.

It was not until the late fourth century that the church even began to actively intervened in funeral rites, with Ambrose of Milan in the 380s and Augustine of Hippo in the 390s intervening against a range of funeral rites, particularly grave-side feasting (Brown 1981, 26). This continued in the first few decades of the fifth century, culminating in Augustine's most considered statement on the burial of dead, with particular reference to burial *ad sanctos*, the *De Cura Gerenda Pro Mortuis* (On the Care to be had for the Dead). In his detailed exploration of Christian burial and the cult of saints, Peter Brown's *The Cult of Saints* (1981) has drawn attention to the use of burials and grave-side rituals by elites as an arena for social competition, or, in John Barrett's terms, a field of discourse (Barrett 2000b). This competition could be through conspicuous consumption and emulation at the grave, or through interventions in the celebrations of cult rituals at the graves of saints (Brown 1981, 23-40). In this period there was an increasing tension between the power of local elites articulated through kinship relations, and the expanding Christian church, an artificial kin-group aiming to supplant pre-existing ties of loyalty to family and replace them with a wider sense of loyalty to the Christian community. In Brown's words '... the strong sense of community preserved by Christian ritual, was only so much icing on the top of a rich and increasingly crumbly cake of well-to-do Christian families' (ibid., 31-1). It is at the grave-side that these tensions crystallised; this contextualises the Church's intervention into an aspects of life and death which had previously been the domain of the family. By preventing ostentatious grave-side ritual, whether at family graves or *ad sanctos,* the Church hoped to prevent the privatisation of this aspect of the holy, and asserted its right to dictate burial practices. The Church also acted to select and cultivate only certain holy graves to create foci of worship controlled by the church rather than lay bodies. Although the Church was starting to assert its rights to intervene in mortuary practice, it had not yet developed a sophisticate theological apparatus to deal with death and burial. In Augustine's opinion funerals and burials were not important for the dead: 'Therefore, all such offices, that is, the care taken with funerals, the embalming for burial, the procession of the mourners, are more for the comfort of the survivors than to assist the dead' (*De Civitate Dei* 1.13) and 'Regardless of what is spent for burying the body it is not an aid to salvation but a duty of our humanity according to that love by which no one ever hated his own flesh' (*De Cura Gerenda Pro Mortuis* 18).

Here we see burial rites changing and becoming incorporated into Christian discourse not as a simple reaction to the shifting religious loyalties of the burial community. Instead, the burial rite is a context in which varying identities (religious and secular) are expressed and contested by competing interest groups. The church's response to competition from secular elites is to extend the contexts within which expression of religious identity is deemed to be important. We are not seeing the spread of religious belief, but rather its articulation in new contexts as a response to socio-political tensions. The challenge is in locating where the boundaries of *religion* lie in the early medieval period; Christian and non-Christian traditions mapped themselves onto society in different ways. The boundaries of the sacred and profane or ritual and secular are not fixed. Indeed the entire notion of this dichotomy may not, as Durkheim implied, be one of the underlying structuring principles of all religions (Durkheim 1976, 37; Brück 1999). Instead there is a requirement to establish how such conceptual divisions are constructed and maintained (Habbe 2006). The techniques of ritualisation may include, among other factors, such diverse phenomena as prayer, votive deposition, the formal structuring of space through architecture or other forms of monumentality, the formal structuring of the body, whether through choreographed movement, as in the liturgy, or through bodily adornment (vestments, hair styles, ritual jewellery) (Bell 1995). The ritualisation of fields of discourse may be extended through all the senses, including the aural (music, singing, silence) and even olfactory (incense, the smells of sacrificial offerings). It is through these ritual activities that the cultural boundaries of religion are generated (Bell 1997, 82-3). The spheres of discourse which may be ritualised in this way are also diverse and include physical space, notions of time, and ideas about personhood and authority. Thus religious identity is ultimately something created and expressed in contextually specific arenas, which are created through the process of ritualisation. In studying the process of conversion, the challenge is to plot the changing processes of ritualisation and explore how they create arenas in which religion is expressed.

Archaeology and the study of religion

While the adoption of an identity approach to the study of early Christianity may give us a theoretical framework in which to place the articulation of belief, there is still a need to consider further the way in which religious identity is expressed in practice. Inevitably when exploring an historic period this

2. Approaching religion: archaeology and belief

leads us to a consideration of the relationship between material culture and text. In recent years the complex relationship between archaeology and history has been increasingly under the lens (e.g. Moreland 2001; Andrén 1998; Norr 1998, 11-14; Price 2002, 25-37). The pervasive influence of the dualistic model of religions can again be seen influencing the relationship between archaeology and the study of religion, with the study of past 'world religions' privileging the role of texts and documents as the key interpretative media, while 'local religions' (for which we can usually read as 'prehistoric' religions) are primarily addressed through archaeology.

Traditional approaches to the study of religion through archaeology were pessimistic. This pessimism was classically expressed in Christopher Hawke's 'Ladder of Inference' which placed matters of belief and spiritual belief as the hardest to access through archaeology (Hawkes 1954), a standpoint which reflected the general attitude of other key figures in Anglophone archaeology in the first half of the twentieth century (cf. Childe 1956, 125-31). The development of processual and systems approaches to archaeology from the 1960s should potentially have engaged with the ideological and symbolic element of society as belief and ideology were often posited as composing one of the sub-systems that comprised society (Insoll 2004, 46-50). However, in practice the primary avenue of research by those using these approaches was via subsistence and exchange, with ideology being ignored and assumed to be epiphenomenal. The representation of societies as essentially homeostatic bounded entities consisting of various sub-components rather than fluid and dynamic groupings also meant that such approaches were ill-adapted to address processes of religious change, whether generated through internal development or external contact. More fundamentally, there was little interest in meaning and social agency in such approaches (Bender et al. 1997, 148). The rise of post-processual approaches to the study of archaeology saw the development of a social archaeology with an increased interest in recovering meaning, bringing the role of religion and ritual in social reproduction more to the

41

fore. Post-processualism was not a coherent school and its development brought about a series of different ways of thinking about religion and ritual in society (Insoll 2004; Fogelin 2008). One such approach was heavily influenced by Marxism and interpreted ritual as creating and promoting power and enacting dominant ideologies (e.g. Parker Pearson 1982; Kristiansen 1984). The more formal expression of Marxist approaches was not widespread, but the wider focus on the relationship between religion and power was an important one. In Britain, the study of prehistoric ritual took a distinctly phenomenological turn, with an increased interest in the subjective experience of monumental architecture (e.g. Tilley 1994; Barrett 1994; Bender 1997). This was connected with a wider reconsideration of long-term landscape continuity (e.g. Bradley 1987). A final key stream was the increased use of structuration theory (as developed by Anthony Giddens) and Pierre Bourdieu's notion of *habitus* as a way of re-introducing the notion of agency into the debate, an area noticeably lacking in processual approaches to archaeology. This lead to an increased interest in small-scale domestic practices, particular depositional practices and the use of domestic space (e.g. Hill 1995; Hodder 1990). These so-called *practice* approaches reaffirmed the importance of repetitive actions and 'embodied knowledge' in re-creating and expressing social structure (Nilsson-Stutz 2006; 2008, 168)

Crucially, however, these developments in theoretical approaches to religion and ritual took place in an almost entirely prehistoric context. Those working in medieval archaeology generally showed little engagement with these important theoretical debates until the early 1990s (for the British context see Gerrard 2003, 219-29; Gilchrist 2009). The reasons for this apparent lack of interest in theoretical approaches to material culture by medievalists are complex, but one key fact was the apparent disciplinary rupture caused by the Roman occupation of Britain, leading to prehistorians and medieval archaeologists developing distinctly separate disciplines. There had been a limited flirtation with processual approaches to early medie-

2. Approaching religion: archaeology and belief

val religion and belief (e.g. Mytum 1989; 1992). Generally processual syntheses of early medieval material studiously avoided dealing with religion and ritual in any depth (e.g. Arnold 1988; Hodges 1982). It was only with the development of post-processualism that medieval archaeologists began to engage with theoretical approaches to religion and ritual more seriously, with important early work including Pam Graves' structuration theory informed exploration of the use of medieval parish churches (Graves 1989). While, intriguingly, the archaeology of Christianity in the second millennium AD appears to have become more theoretically engaged, the archaeology of first-millennium belief (both Christian and pagan) has remained far more traditional in outlook. The only area in which there has been a sustained engagement with theory has been the increased interest in monumentality, particularly monument re-use (e.g. Williams 1997; Semple 1998), although the notion of structured deposition is starting to be explored in more detail (e.g. Petts 2003; Hamerow 2006; Bowles 2007).

A lack of engagement with some aspects of the theoretical debate was not simply a disciplinary issue, with medievalists being slow to bring on board new approaches to archaeology. There were also key variations in approach along national lines. The theoretical synopsis presented so far has been primarily Anglocentric; the shift from culture-history to processualism to post-processualism was a sequence not followed across all of Europe. For a range of reasons Scandinavian archaeology was relatively closely allied with Anglo-American theoretical debates and was early to integrate post-processual approaches (Varenius 1995). Significantly, lacking a period of Roman occupation, there was a more *longue durée* approach taken to the study of religion and ritual in the first millennium AD, with far more interplay between scholars working on areas that in Britain would have been seen as either 'prehistoric' or 'early medieval' (Gilchrist 2009, 388; see Andrén et al. 2006; Jennbert 2000). This tension is caught nicely by Richard Bradley, who has noted: 'Some of the groups who settled in England during the post-Roman period were

43

prehistoric when they left their homelands and Early Medieval when they arrived the other side of the North Sea' (Bradley 2006, 16).

However, while areas of Scandinavia did engage earlier with post-processual approaches to religion, other areas of Europe, despite lacking a Roman 'interlude', retained a far more traditional approach to religion, both pagan and Christian. One key phenomenon was the coincidence of the rise of Romanticism and the emergence of nationalist movements across much of central and eastern Europe in the nineteenth century. This led to a resurgence of interest in 'folklore', in terms of both its contemporary practice and its long-term expression, particularly as a way of defining national identities (e.g. see Jonuks 2005 for a review of folklore and archaeology in Estonia). Methodologically these scholars used oral tradition and philology as their main sources of evidence and dealt with material culture and field monuments in a relatively uncritical manner. In the longer term, East European archaeology mainly utilised a culture-historical approach to establish the time-depth of key ethnic groups (e.g. Buko 2008, 2-10; Curta 2001; Jones 1997, 40-55). The impact of 40 years of Soviet control in many of these areas also limited interest in topics related to belief and ritual, with research instead prioritising research into settlement, subsistence and agriculture and the development of specific modes of production (particularly feudalism), although there was still an extremely strong interest in ethnic history (for Estonia see Mäesalu and Valk 2006, 136-50; for Poland, Buko 2008, 11-12; for 'Moravia', Curta 2009, 239-40).

Since the end of Soviet control in the early 1990s there has been an increased openness towards post-processual approaches in some countries (Barford 2002; Marciniak 2006). However, while such approaches have addressed issues related to prehistoric ritual activity, there has still been little theoretical engagement with the archaeology of Christianity and conversion, which has remained within a dominant historical and art historical paradigm. Whether in Britain or elsewhere in Europe there remains an lack of engagement between the archaeology of early Christianity and theoretically aware approaches to the study of ritual. One of the key factors underlying the reluctance of those working on the early Church to engage with religion may be the difficulty of reconciling the study of what is deemed an essentially text-driven or logocentric religion with the study of material culture. In the words of Florin Curta: 'To many archaeologists working in Eastern Europe in the early medieval period, written records were a substitute for a sound theoretical basis' (Curta 2005, 6).

This gets to the heart of the one of the greatest theoretical challenges for those working on the archaeology of historic periods, the relationship between material culture and text.

Ritual, artefact and text

I recently attended a large multi-village festival for a south Indian deity with a friend of mine. He was asked by one of the young men in the crowd 'Are you a Hindu?'

'No,' he answered. 'I am a Jew.'

'Is a Jew a Hindu?'

'Well they do many similar things.'

'Do you break coconuts and light camphor?'

'No,' he answered

'Then you are not a Hindu.'

Hiltebeitel 1991, 28

This little story crystallises one of the problems faced by the archaeologist studying religion; the relationship between cultural practice and religious belief. As products of a predominantly Judaeo-Christian society, for many of us our default approach to religion is primarily textual, but as this incident makes clear, religion is much more than just texts. The 'archaeological' approach to religion, or, as it is more usually termed in the literature, 'ritual', emphasises materiality (Barrett 1991; 1994, 70-85). This may sound axiomatic; of course archaeology, particularly prehistoric archaeology, is founded on the study of material culture. The danger arises when, because material culture is the only source of evidence, it becomes the only explanatory factor.

John Barrett distinguishes between the knowledge obtainable through everyday action within the world (based on Bourdieu's concept of *habitus*), and a more distanced, abstract theory of knowledge, which he understands through a textual metaphor (Barrett 1994, 80-1; Bloch 1985). For Barrett, one way in which this more distanced knowledge may be articulated is through the ritual process; the ritual is seen as a text having reference to some external supernatural guarantor of truth. However, despite this theoretical separation of the unconscious forms of knowledge embodied by the 'numb imperatives' of *habitus* (Bourdieu 1991, 69) and the explicit didactic nature of ritual, the two are often elided (Gosden 1994, 119). Both forms of knowledge are seen as being played out through encounters with material culture. Barrett particularly focuses on the creation of the spatial aspect of the fields of discourse within which the ritual process is played out (Barrett 1994, 72-7; 2000b, 5-16). Although distanced from day-to-day activity, ritual is tied to material culture. This emphasis on the material aspect of ritual ignores aspects of social memory and performance which do not have physical correlates, such as music, drama, oral culture and, most ironically for a textual metaphor, the content of the texts themselves.

This contrasts with the broadly textual approach taken to the study of Christianity and other so-called world religions. In this approach we see material culture subordinated to textual evidence. Again this is not surprising; Christianity is pre-eminently a religion of the word: *logos*. Other world religions have a similar emphasis on the written word as the fundamental interface between society and God (e.g. Insoll 1999). Whether we are considering the Bible, the Qur'an or the Baghavad Gita, the main texts are all seen as divinely inspired revelations by God of his plan for his followers.

Christianity, Islam and Judaism also have a tradition of using history for didactic purposes: the Old and New Testaments and the Qur'an all focus on the historical foundation of the religion as a means of legitimising their claims to truth. Although small-scale religions may have foundation and creation myths these are often perceived as being outside time. In Christianity recorded history is the arena in which God's divine plan unfolds. Texts are used to establish the links that connect modern worshippers with the founders of their religion. All these religions have rituals that re-enact the key moments in their histories, such as the Haj, Pesach or the Nativity and Easter (e.g. Coleman and Elsner 1995, 56). Christianity and Islam both initially took root in societies where there were pre-existing secular literary historical traditions (Blockley 1981; Lapidus 1988, 91-7). Considering this context it is not surprising that in religions that are so fundamentally historicising that texts should occupy such a central ground in both their history and historiography (e.g. Frend 1996, 1999). In addition the sheer quantity of documentary evidence created in the first centuries of Christianity is staggering, and this mass of data (still being added to: Frend 1999) must also contribute towards the central ground held by documentary evidence.

While this body of data has allowed the history of Christianity to be written with great depth and subtlety, it has also meant that the relationship between textually-derived modes of knowledge and material culture has not been adequately considered. All too often the archaeology of Christianity has served as a mere picturesque backdrop to the bloody internecine conflicts within the early church. The three main dimensions of early Christian archaeology – architectural studies, art and epigraphy – have all, to a greater or lesser extent, relied on a textually derived interpretative framework, focussing for example on the demands of the liturgy.

Such an approach can typically be found in attempts to relate artefacts to objects mentioned in texts (e.g. Frend 1985-6; de Bhaldraithe 1991). A good example of this blindness to the active role of material culture can be found in the study of early church architecture. Much of the work focuses on architectural history and chronological studies. While the best of these studies add greatly to our understanding of the topic, they run the risk of degenerating into an exercise in typology, and when interpretation does occur it is often couched in terms of the demands of the liturgy (e.g. Mainstone 1988; Teteriatnikov 1992; Loosley 1999; Pickles 1999, 5), privileging the textual over the material in matters of interpretation. Very little thought is given to the way in which the social use of space within churches serves to mould the way in which the congregation sees itself and its relationship with ecclesiastical authorities (for an example from a later period see Graves 1989; Gilchrist 1994, 13-14). For example, the vast urban basilicas of late antiquity would have had a very different atmosphere to the small house-churches found on late Roman villas: how does the variation in the size and internal organisation of these buildings affect the congregations who used them (Kilbride 1996)? Instead of liturgy influencing architectural form, does this happen the other way round? As Richard Krautheimer has noted, the great schism between the Orthodox and Catholic Church was presaged by an increasing divergence in architectural form (Krautheimer, 1986, 203-4).

While prehistoric archaeology may overemphasise the material element of society, the archaeology of Christianity frequently seems to ignore the active structuring potential of material culture (Hodder 1986, 118-46), instead using it merely to illustrate what we already know from textual history. One of the few aspects of the archaeology of Christianity which has been considered from a more mainstream archaeological point of view is the role of Christianity in the changing face of late Roman and late antique urbanism (e.g. Carver 1993, 63-7; Orselli 1999; Gauthier 1999; Wharton 1995). This is surely because this is a topic which coincides with more traditional archaeological concerns.

This methodological bind can be avoided if we turn to John Barrett's two models of reproducing knowledge. Rather than seeing text and object as two antithetical types of evidence we should see them both as means of reproducing religious knowledge. As archaeologists we need to explore models of religion that can deal with both textual evidence and archaeological and art historical evidence. We need to see religion as 'dually constructed' (Giddens 1979, 210-12). As the the anthropologist Robert Hefner has written: 'In all religious and ideological discourse there is a dual economy of knowledge, in which explicit doctrinal knowledge is informed by, and mutually informs a less discursive tacit knowledge constructed in a wider social experience' (Hefner 1987, 74-5). There is a recursive relationship between structure and practice. Christianity as a lived religion is functions both as a theoretical structure and a social practice. This model draws archaeology into the analysis in a way that text-based histories of Christianity fail to do. A religion comprises both large-scale symbolic structures and the human practitioners who operate within them: the day-to-day reality of religious practice consists of a dialogue between these two elements.

It is important not to fall into the trap of seeing material culture as simply representing the day-to-day, limited to the realms of *habitus*, nor seeing texts as solely providing the explicit structure of religions (Comaroff and Comaroff 1986, 1-2; Barker 1993, 204; Hefner 1987). Material culture must be read textually, but reciprocally texts must be seen as material culture, as a resource which can be used and deployed in the unconscious ways that are traditionally limited to the material world. More importantly, the two cannot be kept separate. Are religious ceremonies physical expressions of textual liturgy or is liturgy a textual mapping of physical ritual? There is, of course, no correct answer; liturgy cannot exist without theory or practice. While liturgy and ceremony may act explicitly to outline doctrine, the use of the body, space and temporal rhythms within the mass all serve unconsciously to maintain a host of other more subtle religious beliefs. Within the liturgy and mass are structure and practice; there is both distanced ritual and bodily *habitus*.

Such an approach allows us to begin to deconstruct the simplistic models of world/local religions presented at the beginning of this chapter by addressing one of the key oppositions presented – that of text *versus* material culture. As has been shown, this dichotomy has had a pernicious influence on the study of Christianity; with approaches to the archaeology of pre-Christian archaeology being dominated by an archaeological paradigm while the study of Christianity itself has instead been dominated by a text-driven approach (see Chapter 1). Ironically, the analysis of religious conversion, which is predicated on an analysis of new differing world views, has itself been underlain by a similar confrontation between these two approaches to the study of religion. If we want to take an identity approach to the study of religion it is important to undermine this dichotomy, as one of the key dynamics underlying the use of religion to express identity is the configuration of power and authority (Bell 1997, 82). If 'fields of discourse' whether they be a grave, a church or a burial mound, are to be locations where identities can be expressed, maintained or repressed, then much depends on such power; power can prevent or enable such expressions through physical force (such as preventing or limiting access to a location) or through ideological or social sanction (the threat of excommunication, for example). By acknowledging that power can be expressed and legitimated through recourse to both textual authority (particularly the Bible) and material culture (architecture, dress items, etc.), as well as other extra-somatic means, such as personal ties and obligations (of kinship or patronage), we open up a way to explore the process of conversion. These structures of power are not simply reproduced uncritically through ritual practice; instead religious activity can be seen to create and maintain meaning and structure itself; the locus of power is no longer focused on the text, but on all aspects of religious life (Bell 1992, 82). Finally, by extending the emphasis on practice in the study of prehistoric ritual into the domain of Christianity, and bringing our analyses to bear on small-scale and repetitive ritual actions, we can begin to move away from an understanding of religious change that is focused on monumentality and the elite.

3

Christianity and text

In the beginning was the word.

John 1:1

The intimate connection between Christianity and literacy is
often seen as one of the defining features of the first encounter
with the new religion. In an early medieval world that was
largely (and often incorrectly) defined as illiterate, the advent
of Christianity was perceived as being coterminous with the
introduction of literacy. Indeed, it is the administrative potential of literacy that is frequently emphasised as being one of the
key underlying components of Christianity that caused it to be
a catalyst for the consolidation of early kingdoms (see Chapter
1). It is of course possible to challenge this characterisation of
early medieval society. While some groups, such as the Anglo-
Saxons, were undoubtedly non-literate, there appears to have
been a sliding scale of literacy in many regions. In areas such
as western Britain, which had been strongly Romanised, there
are good reasons to argue that there was a continuity of literacy
into the post-Roman period. Some have emphasised the role of
Christianity in maintaining these existing standards of literacy. Taking the works of Patrick and Gildas as an example,
their clearly Christian moralising output shows wide evidence
for the authors being familiar with both Christian patristics
and secular classical learning (Lapidge 1984). The general assumption has always been that this learning was acquired in a
Christian context, probably a monastic school. However, there
is a danger in turning the presence of literacy in a Christian
context into an argument against the continuation of secular

51

literacy, and we must be alive to other possibilities. Patrick tells us himself that his father was a decurion, a member of a Roman town council, as well as a deacon (*Confessio* 1). The administrative duties of a member of a Roman curia would certainly have demanded some level of literacy, and there is no reason to think that such literacy would have been taught only in an ecclesiastical context. Wendy Davies has also suggested that the distinctively Insular Celtic charter tradition, though most apparent in charters produced in an ecclesiastical milieu, probably had its origins in late Roman vulgar (secular) land law (Davies 1982, 274-5). Even the limited archaeological evidence for literacy in sub-Roman Britain comes from secular contexts; the only two styli recovered from known contexts were found in secular contexts (Rahtz et al. 1992, 119-20; Alcock 1963, 119). While the church may have become the ultimate custodian of literacy in early medieval Western Britain, it was clearly building on an existing secular tradition of literacy which may well have continued well into the fifth century.

If one moves focus away from areas of former Romanisation, there is a penumbra of what might be termed para-literacy, with the use of ogham in Ireland and variations of runic script in Scandinavia. Neither script is an entirely pristine development, and both clearly have links to external, probably classical, systems of graphemes and grammatical systems (Moltke 1985; McManus 1997). However, the Scandinavian use of runes was clearly originally developed entirely outside a Christian context, and while the use of ogham is often linked to the rise of Christianity in Ireland, there is in fact no explicit connection between the two. The chronology of ogham as currently understood certainly allows for it to have developed at a time before it is generally accepted that Christianity arrived in Ireland.

The ways in which runic and ogham scripts were used, however, varies widely. Certainly in Ireland the surviving evidence suggests they were used epigraphically on stones with some element of commemorative function, although they may also have been used for other purposes. The evidence for use of ogham on personal items is relatively late and limited (e.g. Forsyth 2007). This is in contrast to early evidence for runes, which although used widely as an epigraphic script, also appears far more widely on portable objects, indicating their use for purposes of 'pragmatic literacy'. This can be seen in the huge range of rune-inscribed sticks from Norway including commercial communications, personal messages and religious phrases (Spurkland 2001). While much of the evidence for this more practical side of runic literacy is relatively late, this may be more due to matters of preservation, and the record that Anskar brought Louis the Pious a letter written in runes may be a reflection of a more extensive use of runes than is generally appreciated (*Vita Ansgarii* 12, 24). This is a clear reminder that monolithic notions of 'literacy' risk hiding widespread variation in its actual day-to-day use. While, as seen above, it is possible to criticise the close conceptual link between Christianity and literacy on purely positivist grounds, highlighting the presence of pre- or non-Christian literacy in the early medieval world, it is important to begin to dismantle the entire notion of a unified 'package' of literacy as used within and between early medieval societies. Within societies, it is clear that different modes of literacy could be deployed at different times and in different ways. This can be recognised most clearly in Scandinavian societies where the advent of Christianity did not lead to the ousting of runic literacy. Instead, there are parallel discourses of Latin and runic literate traditions which operated within a different range of registers and were materialised in a different range of media (Spurkland 2001). Even churchmen could be proficient in the use of both Latin and runes, and there is a substantial body of ecclesiastical runacy (Moltke 1985, 407-500). Between societies it is also possible to recognise different traditions in documentation – for example, early medieval Ireland produced a large number of legal texts, despite the notable lack of 'pragmatic' legal documents, such as charters, *placita* and dispute resolutions, which are however are found widely in Anglo-Saxon England, which has produced far fewer law codes (Stacey 2007, 92).

More fundamentally, it is possible to address this issue from the opposite direction and question the extent to which literacy was fundamental or of prime importance to the church. There is nothing uncontroversial in reminding ourselves that in the early medieval and late antique worlds the vast majority of Christians were illiterate. Literacy was generally confined to a relatively small élite. Keith Hopkins has suggested that at the end of the first century there are likely to have been less than fifty adults in the Christian church who could read and write with any fluency, with perhaps only a thousand by the end of the second century (Hopkins 1998). As he notes, 'written Christianity was initially constructed by a tiny group of socially marginal men' (Hopkins 1999, 86). Even within the priesthood, the practical grasp of literacy could clearly vary widely; for every Bede or Alcuin, it is likely that there was a priest such as the one met by Boniface whose grasp of Latin was insufficient to recite the central baptismal formula correctly (Emerton 1941, 122, LIV).

While the extent to which literacy could be found in pre-Christian contexts or secular contexts is an interesting topic of exploration, it perhaps misses an underlying issue. The argument for the prime role of literacy within Christianity is not simply about the relatively contingent connection between literacy and the appearance of the church in early medieval contexts. Rather it is connected to the role of the text as a key way in which the early medieval church was structured; ultimately, it is the role of text as the sole mode of authority that is in question. Not surprisingly, the Bible is often highlighted as the ultimate source of authority for Christians. It is seen as the touchstone on which matters of faith and practice were tested and validated. Indeed, Christianity, Islam and Judaism have all been presented as 'religions of the book', as logocentric belief systems that derive ultimate authority from a key holy text. However, this can perhaps be seen as ultimately a rather 'Protestant' understanding of the relationship between the Bible and religious authority, one which privileges the role of texts above other means of establishing and maintaining authority over belief and practice within Christianity. This is not to suggest that the early church did not place the Bible at the centre of belief using the scriptures 'for teaching, for reproof, for correction and for training in righteousness' (2 Timothy 3:16). However, there was always a balance between scriptural authority and the institutional authority of the church; one that was only overthrown by the Reformation principle of *sola scriptura* (scripture alone).

Institutional authority could on a day-to-day basis be expressed in a variety of ways. Documents were certainly an important way in which papal and episcopal demands could be declared, whether through formal papal bulls or the huge amount of correspondence generated by the papacy, such as the letters that went between Augustine and Gregory the Great connected to the conversion of Anglo-Saxon England. However, authority could also be expressed and maintained in other ways. There was undoubted personal authority exercised through key individuals, both by virtue of their institutional rank within the church, but also through personal charisma. The latter comes through strongly in records of individuals such as Martin of Tours, who clearly often had ambiguous relationships with the formal ecclesiastical hierarchy but none the less were able to exercise considerable influence on religious belief and practice within their sphere of influence. Peter Brown has written extensively about the key role as social mediators and entrepreneurs assumed by late antique holy men acting as honest brokers in local secular, as well as religious, disputes (Brown 1971). Their authority to act in this manner was not derived from or defended by reference to the Bible, but was instead predicated on their own personal example and their direct, often viscerally physical, engagement with devotional practices.

A final and profoundly important source of religious authority in the early medieval period was, of course, custom or practice. Appeals to the authority of tradition were a key strategy in ecclesiastical disputes. This can be seen explicitly in Bede's record of the Synod of Whitby (664 AD) where the Irish and Anglo-Saxon churches met to address matters of disagreement in church matters. One of the key issues of debate was the means of calculating the date of Easter. Crucially, both parties appealed not to the Bible to support their arguments, but to tradition; according to the Irish bishop Colman, 'The Easter customs which I observe were taught me by my superiors, who sent me here as bishop, and all our forefathers, men beloved of God, are known to have observed these customs', while Wilfrid claimed that 'Our Easter customs are those that we have seen universally observed in Rome ... we have see the same customs generally observed throughout Italy and Gaul when we travelled through these countries for study and prayer' (*HE* III.25). Here we can see authority being expressed through traditions passed on by personal contacts and relationships. This has important lessons for those attempting to develop an archaeological approach to the study of Christianity. Great care has to be taken to avoid privileging the documentary record over other the material record in considering and understanding early medieval Christianity. The Bible and other documentary sources cannot be used in a simple way to 'test' the extent to which a particular aspect of Christianity conformed to accepted norms. Instead, other forms of authority, of custom, of person, of tradition existed alongside textual authority; in some situations these may have complimented the documentary record, but in other cases they have the potential to compete with and oppose the written word. Crucially, this brings us back to the model for early medieval Christianity developed in the previous chapter; religion was dually constructed, relying on the explicit articulation of belief and practice as expressed through the texts, but also being constituted through practice (tradition; custom). If we characterise the early church as logocentric, we risk failing to deal adequately with the material expressions of belief that are addressed by archaeologists. These material expressions do not survive simply as embodiments of belief as expressed in the written word, but actively contributed in a positive and creative manner to the development of early medieval Christianity.

3. Christianity and text

The rest of this chapter will try and explore the way in which the way in which material dimensions of early medieval Christianity might be interpreted, drawing on some of the ideas developed above and in previous chapters. Through a series of case studies, it will be shown how, with an increased emphasis on archaeology and, more generally, the materiality of religious belief, it is possible to develop increasingly subtle understandings of how religious belief could be expressed. There is nothing novel in emphasising that for the majority of the population of early medieval Christendom, the experience of religious education and worship would have been entirely non-literate. Even for members of the literate clergy, much devotional activity would not have engaged directly with written texts; at the very core of Christian worship, the celebration of the mass, the majority of the action involved a performance with a complex script of memorised utterances (liturgy) and sequences of ritualised gestures and movement.

Catherine Bell emphasises the importance of 'framing devices' in defining ritual action, structured distinctions in behaviour and action that act to distance 'ritual' behaviour from actions that could be considered secular or profane (Bell 1997). This act of framing can be seen in the way in which the notion of 'liturgy' as a distinct constellation of ritual acts was separated out from other Christian religious activity. The core liturgical act in Christianity, the celebration of the Eucharist, required some degree of spatial framing, primarily the presence of an altar; generally, this is most likely to have occurred within a clearly defined church structure. However, small portable altars attest to the fact that the presence of an altar could itself act as an appropriate 'frame' that could transform any location into an area appropriate for the celebration of the Eucharist. Another key way in which liturgy was framed in the Western church was through the use of Latin rather than the local vernacular tongue. While in some late antique contexts, the use of Latin would not have distinguished the expression of the Eucharist from day-to-day speech, in much of the medieval world, the act of code switching would have acted as a framing

device distinguishing these sacred utterances from more pro-
saic behaviour. Even though the majority of an early medieval
congregation is unlikely to have been sufficiently fluent in
Latin to have understood the content of the liturgy, the use of a
distinctly different language would have marked it out as a
clearly sacred act.

The use of Latin may well have been just one of a range of
linguistic codes used within early medieval societies; for example, in early medieval Ireland customary or vernacular
language (*gnáthbérla*) was distinguished from other versions of
Irish that were marked by atypical grammatical structures or
a different vocabulary, such as *bérla Féne* ('legal language') and
bérla na filed ('language of the poets'), as well as different
languages, specifically *bérla bán* ('white language'), that is,
Latin (Stacey 2007, 99). Other framing devices might include
the wearing of specific items of clothing (vestments), the deployment of particular bodily postures, such as the *orans*
position, even specific sounds (bells; chanting) and smells (incense). All of these would have acted to define and regulate the
celebration of liturgical acts. Significantly, the successful enac-
tion of liturgy required the appropriate framing devices to be
put in place. Indeed the appropriate use of framing devices
could become a point of contestation – an early sixth-century
letter to two Breton priests from three Gallic bishops condemns
the use of portable altars, making it clear that this, along with
the presence of women assisting the celebration, made the act
invalid (Howlett 1995, 66-72). In essence, for these key ritual
activities to be correctly carried out it was not simply a case of
correctly reciting the relevant texts, they had to be appropri-
ately materialised and performed.

A second key element of Bell's definition of a 'frame' is the
notion that they also acted '[to] create a complete and con-
densed, if somewhat artificial world ... a type of microcosmic
portrayal of the macrocosm' (Bell 1997, 160). One might question how far the ritual acted as a reflection of the existing
cosmic and social structure, rather than expressing an ideal or
anticipated outcome of the act, and elsewhere she herself notes

that ritual was not merely the 'dramatizing or enacting of prior conceptual entities' – it is rather, active and ongoing reformulation of belief (Bell 1997, 38). However, it is clear that liturgical action could be used not just to bring communities together, but also explore and express the divisions and structuring principles that pervaded them. For example, within the liturgy there is a basic distinction between those who celebrate the act itself (the clergy) and those who attend and witness its celebration (the congregation). Both groups can be further distinguished: only ordained priests can say the Eucharistic prayer, although deacons can read the gospel – this is what Robin Chapman Stacey has called 'restrictions on performative speech' (Stacey 2007, 105). There were also clear distinctions within the congregation – catechumens had to leave the church before the creed and Eucharistic prayer, while those who had been baptised could attend the entire service (Yarnold 1978). These divisions could be reflected physically and were often mapped out spatially within church structures. The zone of activity of the clergy was the sanctuary, indicated by the presence of the altar, and often defined by a screen (*cancelli*). There was also often a distinct *ambo* for preaching. The body of the congregation would attend within the body of the nave, while in some traditions the presence of a western narthex acted as a zone to which catechumens could withdraw at the appropriate point (Krautheimer 1986). Further distinctions might be played out within buildings; the seventh-century Irish *Liber Angeli* refers to ecclesiastics being allowed to offer praise in the southern basilica in Armagh, while others were merely allowed to listen in the northern basilica (Stacey 2007, 105). Gender roles might also be reflected through the use of space. Cogitosus' description of the basilica of St Brigit in Kildare records separate entrances for men and women, going on to state, 'And so, in one vast basilica, a large congregation of people varying in status, rank, sex and local origin, with partitions placed between them prays to the omnipotent Master, differing in status, but one in spirit' (Conolly and Picard 1987, 25-6).

While these specific framing devices served to materialise
Christian ritual, defining it and validating it, they did not
entirely separate religious activity from a range of other formalised or ritualised activities and practices in the early
medieval world. As already noted above, in early medieval
Ireland, linguistic code switching was also used to mark out
distinct legal and poetic discourses, and distinguish them from
vernacular actions. There was often a close intersection between ecclesiastical and legal practices, such as cursing, oaths
and compurgation, and ordeals. These intersections might take
the form of swearing on relics. For example, within in medieval
Welsh legal traditions, the use of relics to authenticate oaths
was a common one. When an individual who had stood surety
for another wished to deny a claim by a debtor he was required
to declare 'By the relic which is here, I am a surety from you for
what is said, and falsely have you sworn ...', while the debtor
placed his lips to the relic (Jenkins 2000, 64). A man who
wished to deny having had sexual intercourse with a woman 'in
bush and brake' was required to swear on a 'bell without a
clapper' (Pryce 1993, 43). The twelfth-century saints' lives
also record a similar use for relics; the *Vita Cadoci* notes the
use of Gildas' bell for swearing oaths (*Vita Cadoci* 27). The
relationship between legal activity and religious activity
might be more subtle; for example an Anglo-Saxon Rogationtide homily compares the stations of the Rogationtide
processions with *gemotstow* (legal meeting places) (Bedingfield 2002, 225).

Underlying these similarities in framing strategies is an
underlying similarity in many ritual aspects of early medieval
society – the emphasis on performance. The significance of the
dramatic and performative aspect of early medieval ritual has
been noted elsewhere, with reference to liturgy (e.g. Bedingfield 2002) and law (e.g. Stacey 2007). According to Flanigan,
Ashley and Sheingorn (2005, 652), 'To do justice to the histori-
cally complex realities of medieval liturgy, we need to begin
viewing it as the cultural site for the most inclusive social and
political as well as religious performance.' This performative

element of early medieval ritual behaviour, whether following a pre-determined script (e.g. liturgy) or the articulation of unique acts within defined parameters, has led Robin Chapman Stacey to describe the practice of law in early medieval Ireland as 'an intersection of artistry, technical skill and politics' (Stacey 2007, 77). However, it is important to remember that performance is not simply an oral phenomenon; whether a theatrical piece or a religious ritual, the appropriate frames are required to ensure that it is understood correctly. The lack of these frames, or more importantly in a conversion situation, the lack of a commonly agreed set of frames, can lead to misunderstandings or worse. A wonderful example of this can be found in the *Chronicle of Henry of Livonia*, describing attempts by Albert, Bishop of Riga, to win converts from among local pagans:

> That same winter a very elaborate play of the prophets was performed in the middle of Riga in order that the pagans might learn the rudiments of the Christian faith by an ocular demonstration. The subject of this play was most diligently explained to both converts and pagans through an interpreter. When however, the army of Gideon fought the philistines the pagans began to take flight, fearing lest they be killed, but were quietly called back (*Chronicle of Henry of Livonia* IX (14)).

Despite the presence of an interpreter to explain the action, a lack of the shared appreciation about dramatic framing conventions between the Christian Germans and the pagan Livonians led to misunderstanding. Crucially for archaeologists, many of these framing devices, particularly the structured use of space and artefacts, are particularly accessible to those exploring material culture and the built environment. The failure to factor these contexts into analyses of early medieval ritual activity can lead to only a partial picture of these activities being reached.

Case study: votive deposition in Roman Britain

A consideration of the earliest period of Christianity in Britain provides us with an opportunity to explain the way in which the process of ritualisation can be conceptualised. One of the particular features of Romano-British Christianity is the presence of a distinct series of large lead vessels or tanks with a clear ritual function found across the lowland area of the province (Petts 2003, 96-9). While some of these carry only a very simple decorative scheme, others carry diagnostically Christian symbols, including the *chi-rho* symbol, often shown accompanied by the alpha and omega; other decorative images include simple figures in an *orans* position commonly associated with early Christian worship, and in one example, from Walesby in Lincolnshire, what appears to be a ritual washing or bathing scene, most likely a baptism by immersion (Thomas 1981, 221-4). The ritual function of these vessels has, not surprisingly, been a focus of debate centring on whether they were intended primarily to act as fonts or fulfilled some other purpose associated with ritual ablution, such as *pedilavium*, a foot-washing ritual (Watts 1991, 71-3). Ultimately this debate revolved around taking an item of material culture and attempting to link it to a recognised role within the Christian liturgy. Crucially, such approaches fundamentally decontextualise these items, focusing on form and using it to construct meaning. While this quest for ritual function is not an unworthy one, its failure to take a contextual approach to these items does not address other potential ways in which the lead tanks could have derived their ritual significance. This can be seen by analysing the range of locations in which the artefacts have been discovered.

While some such tanks are random finds with no clear context, a significant number are known to come from watery locations; those from Ashton (Northamptonshire) and Caversham (Berkshire) came from wells, one from Heathrow was located at the top of a waterhole, and a number of others were discovered in rivers or fens. Overall, where a precise location is known for their discovery, the majority come from watery contexts (Petts 2003b). A similar pattern is also found in the deposition of pewter objects with Christian symbols on them, including a hoard of pewter vessels from Heybridge (Essex) and a pewter bowl with a *chi-rho* found on the bed of the Old Welney River (Cambridgeshire) (Thomas 1981, 123).

This consistency begins to suggest that there is some element of formalised structure to the depositional practices that have led to the tanks entering the archaeological record. It is difficult to account for a purely functional factor that might explain this pattern, and the formality and consistency of the pattern can be likened to the kind of practices that Catherine Bell has argued might constitute the process of ritualisation. Thus we might decide to conclude our analysis by noting that the lead tanks can be ascribed a ritual function not only on the basis of their symbolic decorative schemes, but also through the formalisation of their deposition. However, this does not begin to grapple with the relationship between Christian and non-Christian religious activity in late Roman Britain. Christian behaviour in this context did not constitute itself in a vacuum. Instead, the formalisation of Christian ritual behaviour developed within a wider landscape of contemporary non-Christian practice. By an act of further contextualisation it is possible to understand this relationship better. It is clear that the kind of watery context associated with Christian lead tanks was also associated with a range of other ritualised behaviour in Roman and Iron Age Britain over the *longue durée*. A similar pattern of structured deposition in pits, wells and other watery contexts can be found across late prehistoric and Roman Britain and Europe (Bradley 1998b; Brunaux 1988; Ross 1968; Poulton and Scott 1993).

These broad homologies in the placement of tanks and other structured depositional activities can be recognised through a contextual analysis of their placement. It can be seen that the use of watery locations, wells, ditches and rivers as the final destination of these objects constituted a framing device defining the physical act as one with wider ritual connotations. Significantly, the same framing device was used in both 'pagan' and Christian contexts; there is no need to interpret this similarity of activity as some form of syncretic activity or belief system. Instead we see consistency in the repertoire of the underlying structuring principles of religious activity in Roman Britain that transcends notions of pagan or Christian.

It is possible to recognise other areas of consistency or similarity between Christian and non-Christian religious practice in this period, particularly in the placement of votive metal leaves and plaques. The best-known examples are the silver plaques bearing *chi-rho* symbols found in a hoard at Water Newton in Cambridgeshire (Henig 1984, 123-4). These are decorated with Christian imagery, and were found associated with other clearly Christian material, including a vessel carrying an inscription with clear allusions to Eucharistic liturgy (Painter 1999). However, these plaques are part of a wider group of votive items from Roman Britain which were also clearly used in non-Christian ritual, often carrying the name or image of a Roman or native god or goddess (Henig 1984, 145-52). The presence of holes on some of these plaques suggests that they were affixed to an object, presumably located within a temple or shrine. Once again, it is possible to recognise an element of consistency in ritual activity straddling the pagan-Christian divide – the complexity of the nature of framing devices is also recognisable in two ways. First, it is necessary to take an artefact biography approach to the study of these ritual artefacts. In the case of the lead tanks and the votive plaques, their final disposal comes at the end of their use life, the frames used over this period could clearly change; while the use of watery contexts acted as their final frame, they would have been used in alternative contexts before they reached this terminal point in their trajectory. Secondly, one needs to consider the notion that ritual framing devices may even be mutually recursive, acting on and constituting each other as an element with ritual significance. The Christian votive plaques from Water Newton may have been framed by their ritual context (hoard, church or shrine), but equally through their association with other Christian items and their use of Christian imagery, they themselves would have helped to bracket their use contexts as of ritual importance.

In the context of Roman Britain, where the conversion was likely to have been moved forward by individuals from the same broad cultural milieu, there is likely to be a shared understanding of appropriate framing devices and mechanisms that can be used to provide an element of sacrality to an act. While there may be profound differences in the cosmological interpretations and understandings of ritual behaviour, an underlying shared grammar of ritual practice has the potential to provide a shared ground for discourses about change in religious belief. Building on the notions developed by Bergren and Nilsson Stutz (2010), votive deposition can be seen as a shared *strategy* of action. However, in encounters where the two social groups lack this shared set of ground rules about what constitutes ritual behaviour and its boundaries, there is clearly far wider scope for misunderstanding and misinterpretation.

'The word made flesh': the materiality of early Christian text

It has been shown that primacy of text in the structuring of Christian ritual can be questioned and the need for framing devices, often physical, is crucial for the correct operation of ritual activity. Early Christianity was far from text-led; instead its practice was profoundly entangled in materiality. Artefacts and architecture did not simply act as reflections or expressions of text-based rituals, but were fundamentally implicated in the practice of these rituals. It was only through their physical performance, framed by material culture and other sensory and somatic devices, that rituals came into being. However, this does not fundamentally address the underlying opposition between texts and material culture. In recent years though, the complex interaction between texts and material culture has become increasingly problematised (for a recent review of these approaches see Moreland 2006). Moreland emphasises that both text and material culture can be understood in similar ways, both having efficacy or agency within the past, as well as being simple reflections of the past. There is thus a need to understand more closely the intersection of texts and material culture; not just an improved understanding of the generalised ways in which the advent of literacy can be used both as both an instrument of repression and empowerment. At a fundamental level, texts are words made material; turning spoken or thought utterances into material culture. There is a need to better understand the range of ways in which texts are materialised and the different implications these may have.

It is essential to be aware that literacy and orality are not monolithic concepts. Utterances can be expressed in a variety of different ways: spoken, sung or chanted, and I have already touched on the implications of code switching. The importance of the correct or accurate replication of words can also vary widely. In some cases, word-for-word repetition or accuracy is essential, in other situations, it is the general drift or underlying message that is more important. Not surprisingly, there is a wide variety of ways in which words, codes (religious; social; legal) and narratives can be made material. Rather than setting up a simple binary model that opposes text to material culture, it is more useful to recognise numerous spectra in which messages can be encoded, ranging from those that directly materialise specific utterances to those that broadly encode general principles. The axes for these spectra might include such factors as implied or intended discursivity, extent of reproduction, size of intended audience, or linearity of the message (is there a sequential logic to the construction of the message or is it impressionistic?). Individual items may embed material with a range of different strategies; for example, even a manuscript may contain the words of the main text, glosses and emendations, in-text illustrations and marginalia – all with differing purposes and intentions, and each materialised in different ways. The notion of *imagetext*, as developed by W.J.T. Mitchell, is crucial in this respect; this is a recognition that many texts are so reliant on their associated images that neither can be fully understood without the other (Mitchell 1994, 83-107; Brantley 2007, 5-6). In essence it attempts to break down the binary tension of image versus text (for which we might read material culture versus text). The juxtaposition and mutual dependence of text and image must be interpreted as widely as possible. In an early medieval context, art and objects, such as murals, reliquaries, manuscripts and sculpture, which combine text and other images, all benefit from understanding in this way.

A practical way in which this can be seen is on the Ruthwell Cross. This is an eighth-century Anglo-Saxon cross from southwest Scotland that carries one side a series of figurative scenes from the life of Christ (such as the Annunciation and Crucifixion) captioned with Latin inscriptions, while on the other a decorative scheme of inhabited vine scroll is accompanied by excepts from the Anglo-Saxon poem *The Dream of the Rood* in runic script. On this carving, the complex decorative scheme and the associated texts play off each other to create a highly complex monument that embedded communal liturgical action both textually and figuratively. A recent re-analysis of the stone has even argued that the schemes on the cross actively demanded a physical engagement with it through movement in a sunwise decoration, requiring 'onlookers to respond to the cross as a material object, extended in space' (O Carragain 2005, 62).

It is crucial not to see the use of pictorial narratives as an alternative or parallel discourse to textual narratives. Despite Gregory the Great's claim in his Epistle to Bishop Sirenus of Marseilles that 'What writing does for the literate, a picture does for the illiterate looking at it, because the ignorant see in it what they ought to do, those who do not know read it', it is clear that the relationship between words and images is more complex. Images could often be used enhance the engagement with words and texts (Camille 1985; Duggan 1989; Gill 2001); the use of wall paintings and fabric hangings with pictorial images within churches and other ecclesiastical spaces, such as monastic refectories, could interact with other activities, particularly the celebration of the liturgy. This combination of visual and verbal, found also in drama, again brings us back to the performative aspect of ritual and belief. One of the key aspects of text is that it needs to be actualised in some form to have efficacy.

This actualisation of the text may come in a number of ways. The most obvious way is through the act of reading, although this is not a simple or unproblematic concept. One clear area of complexity is in the tension between private or silent reading (although these are not necessarily the same thing) and public reading to an audience or congregation. These distinctions cut across the core material categorisation of texts, such as monumental epigraphy and manuscripts. Inscriptions in stone could be read privately or publicly interpreted, as could codices and books. Underlying these different patterns of use of texts is the extent to which there is an intermediary. For the private reader, there is no necessary intermediary or interpretative voice in the engagement with the text (although marginal notes and glosses could add a layer of interpretation). However, with the public delivery of textual material there is an external human agent between the text and the audience – the mode of delivery might vary, the agent may either provide a strict word-for-word recitation of the text or provide a wider paraphrase or interpretation of the message, or use it simply as a point of departure for a wider exploration or meditation on the relevant themes. In many ways this brings us back to one of the key factors in the discussion of the word and its relationship to Christianity, that of authority. As soon as there is an intermediary in the transition of textual or symbolic material, the audience are required to take the delivery of the message with some element of trust, particularly if they themselves are not literate. This authority of the intermediary might be expressed or recognised in several ways; the spatial context within which the message is delivered, be it pulpit or grave mound, the physical appearance of the individual, whether expressing ecclesiastical authority through the wearing of vestments and the appropriate tonsure or secular authority through haircut, clothes and items of personal adornment. Once again, we see the importance of framing devices in contextualising ritualised activity; for the content of a text to be made effective and its authority to be made real, it is necessary for the correct material conditions to be met.

Case study: texts in stone in early medieval Wales

Christianity in early medieval Wales had its origins in the spread of the church in Roman Britain in the fourth century, and despite its geographical location on the edge of Europe, the early Welsh church was in close contact with other Christian churches on the Continent. One of the earliest classes of evidence connected to the early Welsh church is a group of inscribed stone funerary monuments, usually written in Latin, but sometimes inscribed using both Latin and ogham, with a small number carved in ogham alone (Edwards 2001; Petts 2009, 26-9). The most common formula used on these stones was the phrase HIC IACIT/IACET ('Here lies') along with the name of the deceased accompanied by some information about their ancestry, although some have more extended inscriptions. These stones with Latin epitaphs appear to derive from a widespread late antique epigraphic tradition found widely spread across much of Gaul, Spain and Germany (Handley 2001). Visually there are a number of key features about these Welsh stones. The inscriptions mainly used capital letters (also known as majuscules), the typical style used on Roman monumental inscriptions, with the addition of a range of forms based on Roman written hands, known as uncial (derived from a form of capital letters adapted for non-epigraphic use) and half-uncial (derived from a hand used specifically for writing). The proportion of uncial/half-uncial to capitals increased over time and was probably complete by the mid-seventh century (Tedeschi 1995, 2001). While the quality and regularity of the inscriptions could vary, it is noticeable that apart from the text,

the early stones contain virtually no additional decoration beyond the occasional cartouche, and the stones themselves are
often only crudely shaped. A number of the stones bear crosses,
but it is clear that these were added much later (Longden
2003). In summary, the emphasis on these stones was on the
presentation of the text itself, with little visual distraction. The
choice of burial formula and the letter forms clearly connects
these texts to a monumental epigraphic tradition rather than a
manuscript tradition of textuality. Crucially, with rare excep-
tions, these stones have little about them in form or content
that indicates a clearly Christian identity.

These early stones contrast strongly with a second phase of
Christian monumentality in Wales which comes to the fore
from the seventh century onwards. These are dominated by a
range of cross forms, varying from simple cross-incised stones
to elaborate and substantial free-standing crosses and slab
crosses (Edwards 2001; Petts 2009, 29-35). These crosses are
immediately visually very different from the early stones; they
are usually heavily and elaborately decorated and contain relatively little text. However, even the text that does appear is
presented in a very different way. The first noticeable distinction is the total dominance of half-uncial letter forms, derived
from a manuscript rather than an epigraphic tradition. The
range of formulae and vocabulary used on some stones also
clearly indicates a manuscript model. A good example of this is
apparent on a stone from Llanwnnws (Cardiganshire) (Edwards 2007, CD27). The inscription reads 'CHRISTUS
Q[U]ICUNQ[UE] EXPLICAU[ER]IT H[OC] NO[MEN] DET BENEDIXIONEM
PRO ANIMA HIROIDIL FILIUS CAROTINN' meaning 'Whoever shall
(have) explain(ed) this Name, let him give a blessing for the
soul of Carotinn, son of Hiroidil'. This text has close parallels
with wording used in ninth-century Irish gospels. As well as
showing manuscript influence in the broad wording of this
stone, it can also be recognised in the abbreviations and
contractions used, such as H with a dot over it (for *hoc*) and
N~O~ (for *nomen*); practices which again have clear manuscript origins.

3. Christianity and text

The visual appearance of manuscripts can also be seen to influence the layout and design of some stones. One cross from Llangyfelach (Glamorganshire) depicts a central figure wearing a rectangular tabard (Redknap and Lewis 2005, G52) There is no attempt to depict the drapery accurately, and the rigid shape of the costume resembles the Symbol of St Matthew, from the Book of Durrow (Dublin, Trinity College Library, A.4.5 (57), f. 21v). As well as examples such as this, referencing the layout of manuscript pages, there are even cases where the setting of the inscription appears to imitate the structure of a book. One of the crosses from Llantwit Major has three pairs of panels carrying the inscription. The layout of these panels side by side is reminiscent of an open book or possibly even a wax tablet of the type known to have been used for a range of purposes in the early medieval world, including learning to read and write, as well as potentially acting as notebooks (Charles-Edwards 2003). The materialisation of religious text on these crosses was thus fundamentally different from that on the earlier memorial stones. In these later stones, text was deployed in a way that made strong allusions, visually and in terms of content, to a parallel tradition of manuscript-based textuality, unlike the earlier stones which derive their model of text from a epigraphic tradition. Underlying this may be differing perceptions about authority and text, with the earlier stones deriving textual authority from a tradition which privileged public and monumental texts, whereas the texts on the crosses instead intersect with a textual tradition which draws on the authority of written manuscripts.

A final notable distinction between these later crosses and the earlier inscriptions can be found in the *nature* of the inscriptions. The earlier inscriptions were essentially simple epitaphs, acting as labels marking and memorialising the grave. However, the texts on some of the later crosses, as well as simply memorialising the dead, actively invoked a response or action from the reader. This can be seen on the stone from Llanwnnws noted above. As well as naming the deceased, the stone actively acts as a stimulus for further ritual activity, requesting prayers for the dead. Significantly, the inscription contains the phrase 'Whoever shall (have) explain(ed) this Name ...', which gives a fascinating insight into how these texts were actually perceived. It assumes that most individuals who looked at the stone would not be able to directly understand the text, but instead there was a requirement for further interpretation and explication. For most viewers of the cross, full engagement would thus have been a public act involving an element of performance; the stone appears to have an element of agency, invoking interpretation and further ritual action.

4

Deconstructing paganism

Diu heienschaft ist hochgemuot
'Paganism is proud'
Livonian Rhymed Chronicle, 1.327

In recent years there has been considerable work exploring the pre-Christian religions that were confronted by the first Christian missionaries in Northern Europe (e.g. Price 2002; Carver 2010; Andreen, Jennbert and Raudvere 2006). In general, this has been driven by archaeologists. This is not surprising; there are no surviving first-hand testimonies or records of the process from the convert's perspective, no intimate insights into the tumultuous events to compare with Patrick's *Confessio* or Boniface's letters. However, the many new ways of looking at pagan practice that have been developed have often not percolated through to those exploring the actual process of conversion itself. There has often been a tendency to characterise or stereotype pagan religious practice in certain ways. The all-pervading influence of the binary oppositions used to characterise 'world' and 'local' religions explored in Chapter 2 can again be seen to lead to a series of unwarranted models about the nature of pre-Christian cult behaviour. In general, paganism is seen as small-scale, localised, ritual activity focused around local, often kinship, groupings, using models of cyclical time, reflecting a more general close link to agriculture and nature. Institutionally, pagan religions are seen as being relatively underdeveloped, with few ritual specialists or permanent temple structures. This is in contrast with the international, textually derived Christian church with its well-developed institutional structure of ritual specialists and elaborate sites of worship. Simplistic models of religious change that pit these two caricatures against each other are inevitably going to underplay the complexity of the actual process of religious change. This chapter largely aims to address these conceptions of early medieval European paganism and explore how such models for pagan activity came about.

In Chapter 2 the overarching model of 'world' and 'local' religions was situated within an anthropological tradition that was closely linked to a colonial discourse. Models of non-Christian religiosity were largely modelled in antithesis to the Christian church. However, there was no attempt to address how such models of religions came to be applied explicitly or implicitly to early medieval ritual behaviour. One of the key channels for such characterisation has been the increased use of anthropological models and analogies by historians and archaeologists of this period. Parallels and insights drawn from the work of twentieth-century ethnographers have become increasingly utilised by scholars exploring early medieval religion and religious change. The challenges presented by this anthropological turn were first highlighted by William Kilbride (2000), who suggested that this use of ethnography first appeared in studies of the early medieval world and late antiquity in the late 1980s and early 1990s, although it is possible to trace the use of anthropology to understand early Christianity back to at least the early 1970s in the work of Peter Brown (e.g. Brown 1970; see also Munz 1976). Interestingly, although anthropology has been used by early medieval historians to understand the ritual process more generally, this has largely been applied to interpreting the workings of secular ritual (e.g. Buc 2001).

The extent of the engagement with anthropological writings can vary widely. At one extreme, Henry Mayr-Harting's use of ethnography is limited to a single analogy between the conversion of Mercia and the conversion of the South Sea island of Tikopia inserted into the preface of the second edition of his seminal book on the conversion of Anglo-Saxon England (Mayr-

4. Deconstructing paganism

Harting 1991, 7) – the Pacific parallels were drawn from field-work carried out by Raymond Firth and published in the early 1970s. The work of Robin Horton (1971; 1975) on conversion in South Africa has also attracted a number of early medievalists, including Nick Higham (1997, 8-12; critiqued by Kilbride 2000, 8-12), Lynette Olson (1999) and Carole Cusack (1998, 11-15).

There are, not surprisingly, a number of problems, or at the very least challenges, in the uncritical use of ethnographic parallels to assist in understanding the conversion process. Archaeologists have long recognised the care with which this approach needs to be developed (e.g. Hodder 1982). One key factor is the need to ensure the appropriate degree of contextual similarity between the situation described in the ethnographic material and that with which it is being compared. If the use of an ethnographic analogy is to enhance our understanding of conversion significantly, rather than simply highlight a broad structural similarity or open up a potential interpretation, then it is necessary that care is taken with how they are deployed. As noted in Chapter 2, one of the underlying problems with using anthropological understandings of religion to explore early medieval religious change is that the vast majority of anthropological fieldwork into the transition to Christianity has taken place in a colonial or post-colonial context. In such situations the mutability of religious belief cannot be understood outside the wider social and political developments and tensions created through the process of nineteenth- and twentieth-century colonial contact. In these circumstances, societies are liable to be undergoing profound stress; existing political structures may either be challenged or significantly buttressed and consolidated by new external power structures, existing economic structures may disrupted through the establishment of new border controls and tariff barriers, as well as the underlying economic exploitation of the colonised society (including the introduction of new agricultural crops and techniques). There are also likely to be major inequalities in scientific, medical and military technology between coloniser and colonised. Added to this, there are also usually strong

75

social, political and economic ties between missionary groups and ruling western powers. All this means that the landscape within which religious change occurs in colonial societies is going to be profoundly different to that of the early medieval world. This wider challenge to the use of ethnography by archaeologists has been recently noted by Matthew Spriggs, who has highlighted that many of the concepts drawn from anthropological work on the Pacific by British archaeologists, such as the 'Big Man' and the *kula* ring, are in fact themselves primarily products of the direct and indirect impact of colonial powers in the Pacific (Spriggs 2008). To this we must add the more immediate fact that much early ethnographic work was carried out by missionaries who had a vested interest in the way in which indigenous religious activity was characterised.

All this means that immense care needs to be exercised in the use of anthropological analogy. For example, Robert Markus uses Terence Ranger's study of twentieth-century white settlers in Zimbabwe to understand Christian appropriation of space in the late antique world, arguing that 'Like so many white settlers they had to impose their own religious topography on a territory which they read as a blank surface, ignoring its previous religious landmarks and divisions' (Markus 1990, 142, citing Ranger 1987). This conclusion is simply not borne out by a detailed consideration of the archaeological material, which recognises a close and complex reading and engagement with non-Christian sacred sites by early Christian communities (e.g. Clay 2008). Equally, one might question Lynette Olson's development of Robin Horton's notion of the importance of the clash of microcosmic and macrocosmic world views as an element of the conversion process (1999). While the linked process of colonialism, globalisation and conversion may have provoked a clash of local and internationalising cosmologies in the context of nineteenth- and twentieth-century Africa, it remains doubtful that there was the same clash of perception in the context of missionaries arriving in a 'pagan' territory from a neighbouring kingdom with broadly the same levels of technology. Even in the fifth and sixth centuries, there was extensive communication across Europe between local and regional elites, and the movement of populations and individuals, whether through intentional or forced migration, short-distance raiding, long-distance warfare, trade, exchange or diplomacy means it is unlikely that even when non-Christian beliefs were embedded in a purely local landscape (and more on this below) there was no sense of a wider cognitive landscape within which local peoples were situated.

In addition to the impact of anthropology on the characterisation of pagan religions and the process of religious change, there is a second filter through which pagan religions and practices have been characterised, this time not by modern scholars, but by early medieval Christians themselves. It has been noted elsewhere in this book that all the contemporary descriptions of pagan religiosity come from Christian writers (Bartlett 2007). While some of these writers, such as Boniface, may have directly encountered pagan religious activity, others will have been drawing on second-hand reports and general characterisation. Crucially, much of this will have been seen through the lens of the Bible. While in the preceding chapter I have tried to problematise the priority given to texts and literacy in the practice of Christianity, I would certainly not claim that the Christian engagement with its scriptures was not of profound and fundamental importance in forging an understanding of human society and its wider cosmological and theological position. It is no surprise that the Bible, particularly the Old Testament, contains many descriptions of non-Abrahamic religious practices. I would argue that these provided a powerful model for describing early medieval pagan practice. This was particularly due to the regular use of Biblical events as precedents, allegories and justifications for religious conversions. The majority of early medieval scholars did not read the Bible simply in a literal way as a description of events; rather, following the exegetical approach developed by Origen and others in the second and third centuries AD, they emphasised a deeper spiritual reading of the Bible, which made great play of recognising and tracing parallels and allegories in the Bible to establish deeper truths. There was also a focus on the importance of the Old Testament in presaging the events of the New Testament, the former as a history of disaster recapitulated in the latter as a history of salvation (Reventlow 2001, 172). As a consequence, encounters with paganism by the Israelites in the Old Testament could be seen as prefiguring later Christian encounters with paganism.

A range of practices were characterised in the Bible as pagan, including ritual prostitution and child sacrifice. However, the Hebrew term "aboddh zarah' meaning 'strange/unprescribed rites' has generally been translated as idolatry, and indeed the main way in which the Bible represented inappropriate ritual behaviour was as the worship of idols (Faur 1978). This was in contrast to the Judaic tradition which placed relatively little emphasis on the physical depiction of God; while the use of images was not absent, their deployment was circumscribed. The notion of right or correct cult was clearly laid out in part in the Ten Commandments (Exodus 20:2-17; Deuteronomy 5:6-22), the second commandment being a clear condemnation of idol worship.

Pagans were clearly seen as worshipping idols, such as in Hosea 4:12, which in the Vulgate version reads *'populus meus in ligno suo interrogavit et baculus eius adnuntiavit'* (which can be translated as 'my people worship wood and are answered by a stick'). In some cases idols could be placed in a wooded grove (e.g. 1 Kings 15:13; 2 Kings 17:16) and the sanctuary of the god Baal was associated with a grove (e.g. Judges 6:30) – the planting of a grove close to a Jewish altar was also forbidden (Deuteronomy 16:21). It is no surprise therefore that these tropes and images used to describe pagan cult worship in the Bible should be used to describe early medieval paganism. For example, the description of Pomeranian paganism ascribed to Otto of Bamberg by Herbord specifically mentions 'graven images' (*sculptilia*) using the same term used in the Vulgate to describe idols (Herbord II.30; Deuteronomy 7:5, 7:25; 2 Kings 5:2; Psalm 96:7). Elsewhere, descriptions of pagan lands refer

4. Deconstructing paganism

widely to the practice of 'idolatry' (e.g. *HE* IV.16; *Vita Bonifatii* 6). Groves were regularly depicted as being the location of pagan activity and were regularly destroyed by Christian missionaries; Wigbert of Merseburg destroyed the grove of Schkeitbar (*Chronicon* VI.37) and Boniface famously cut down the sacred oak at Geismar (*Vita Bonifatii* 6); the juxtaposition of a temple and a grove at Uppsala may certainly be based in fact, but it also calls to mind the temple and grove of Baal. In a description of a destruction of a pagan Livonian temple and grove by Henry of Livonia, he used the term '*imagines et similitudines*' ('images and likenesses'), another direct quote from the Bible (Deuteronomy 1:26) (Jonuks 2009). Other biblical imagery could be used to describe pagan practice; Snorri Sturluson's account of the sacrifices at Lade, with the sprinkling of blood on the altar, appears to be directly drawn from rituals depicted in Exodus 24.

This is not to suggest that non-Christian communities did not use figurative representations of humans or animals as a focus for worship, nor that groves, woods and forests could not be utilised as places for ritual activity. Rather, that any description of such practices was inevitably refracted through the lens of biblical images of unorthodox religious practices. The complexity of this situation can be recognised in the descriptions of pagan cult activity at Arkona on the Baltic island of Rügen. A description by Saxo Grammaticus records the placement of liquid in a horn and the measurement of its evaporation after a year as a predictor of the success of a harvest; this is repeated by William of Malmesbury, who added the detail that the liquid was water and honey and that it was part of the worship of Fortuna. Crucially, William observes that St Jerome's commentary on a passage in Isaiah confirms that 'Egyptians and almost all eastern peoples did the same', and it was used to predict the scale of future harvest (Bartlett 2007, 51; Slupecki and Zaroff 1999). The passage from Isaiah itself reads: 'you who have abandoned the Lord, who have forgotten my sacred mountain, who place a table for *Fortuna* and pour out libations upon it' (Isaiah 65:11). In this case it is easy to see how early medieval pagan activity could become reinterpreted within the context of biblical models of paganism. One of the key problems in such descriptions, however, is the focus on the externals of pagan practice, rather than the details of pagan religious beliefs. This indicates a keen interest in the early writers in the niceties of correct behaviour, which was as important as, if not more than, correct belief. This does, though, make it extremely difficult to understand the complexities of non-Christian ethical belief and cosmography. It is important to be aware of our lack of understanding in this context, as characterisation of pagan beliefs regularly includes such key factors as a cyclical rather than a linear conception of time, a lack of a clear ethical framework, and a world-accepting rather than a world-rejecting attitude (e.g. Urbanczyk 2003).

A final filter through which pagan activity has been filtered is via the socio-political uses to which the notion of paganism has been put by post-medieval writers and scholars. Tonno Jonuks has explored the way in which the understanding of the Estonian holy sites know as *hiis* have been characterised from the eighteenth century to the early twenty-first century (Jonuks 2009). He has shown that in the nineteenth century the interpretation of Estonian paganism was closely linked to the generation and definition of a distinct Estonian national identity, which led to an emphasis on the purity of Estonian paganism, undiluted by external influence and the construction of a defined pantheon of deities. In a different context, Howard Williams and Sue Content have demonstrated that the 'paganism' of early Anglo-Saxon society was regularly subordinated to wider narratives about this period, particularly those connected to national origin myths linked to migration (Content and Williams 2010).

Perhaps one of the most important common ways in which pagan religions have been characterised, in an early medieval context, is that they are small-scale. These religious practices are deemed to be inherently local in focus. They are believed to be narrow in scope and interested only in a tightly defined arena. Robin Horton in his study of conversion in Africa char-

4. Deconstructing paganism

acterised local traditional African religions in this way and suggested they were essentially interested in 'the microcosm of the local community' (Horton 1971, 101); he argued that in such societies most people had little interest in the wider macrocosm. While Horton emphasised the geographic dimension to the native microcosm, there is a wider tendancy to characterise traditional religions as in thrall to notions of cyclical time, providing them with very limited chronologocal horizons. Horton's model of microcosmic traditional societies has been criticised by other anthropologists, who have argued that African religions and other institutions were not as bounded as Horton suggested (Hefner 1993a, 20-2; Ranger 1993). In the rest of this chapter I want to develop this critique and argue that our conception of pagan religions as microcosmic in space and time is mistaken. I want to suggest that pre-Christian cosmology was far more wide-ranging than often suggested. By demonstrating that such religions could potentially operate at a variety of scales, not just the local, I argue that models of conversion based on simplistic models of pagan practice need to be re-assessed.

Perceptions of time

One of the key distinctions regularly made between Christianity and paganism is the notion that the former emphasises 'linear time' while pagan societies are embedded in cyclical time (e.g. Urbanczyk 2003; Driscoll 1988; 1998, 154-5). This assumes that pre-Christian societies were primarily predicated on a model of time that emphasised its cyclical and repeating nature, with its close connection to seasonality and agricultural and human reproduction, and no real sense of progress or time depth. Whereas Christianity is closely connected to a linear sense of time, with an historical sense of the past and a clear notion of prospective or future time. This is seen as resulting partly from Christianity's close connection with literacy, which is deemed to facilitate notions of historical time (e.g. Goody 1977), but also from the strong eschatological and salvationary theology inherent within Christianity, which has a clearly developed narrative linked to creation and the final judgement.

However, once again, such simple dyads are far too limiting. This distinction between societies with 'cyclical' and 'linear' time goes back to the work of anthropologists in the early and mid-twentieth century, such as Evans-Pritchard and Levi-Strauss (Lucas 2005, 63-4), and has been heavily critiqued by later anthropologists (e.g. Bloch 1977; Gell 1992). Instead, most anthropologists would accept that all societies operate using a range of different models of time, or *chronotypes*. Indeed, it is generally acknowledged that Christianity has a strong cyclical aspect, seen most strongly in the yearly celebration of the liturgical cycle. Equally, it is increasingly clear that for wider Christian society, the widespread adoption of 'linear time' was a very slow one (Mytum 2006; Burke 1969). In general, the developing subtlety of this debate has focused on expanding and exploring the range of *chronotypes* utilised in Christian society. On the whole, pagan societies appear to be condemned to endlessly repeat themselves, limited to a cyclical conception of chronology. This sets the scene for a profound culture clash when pagan societies and Christian missionaries come into conflict. Perhaps, though, it is also possible to widen our notion of how pre-Christian societies engaged with the passage of time. Early medieval societies clearly did not have a sense that there was no change; the regular appearance of migration and origin narratives in early medieval literature indicates that there was a perception of history, even if the actual chronology may have been imprecise.

This can be seen most clearly in the sphere of burial archaeology. It is perhaps possible to recognise at least two forms of broadly historical time through the archaeological record (cf. Wessman 2010; Gosden and Lock 1998). On one hand there is a sense of past that emphasises links to a deep or mythic past, a chronological sense that cultivates a sense of long-term continuities with an ancestral past. This deep past could be the location of mythological cycles and the activity of legendary heroes. However, there may be less sense of the internal differentiation of time within these fictive eras; in some cases there may be a clear narrative event, such as a migration or other population movement that marks the division between the deep past and the more recent past. This notion of discontinuity or rupture is important, and it brings us to Richard Bradley's work on continuity of ritual activity on prehistoric monuments (1987, 2002). He has emphasised the extent to which monuments of earlier eras have been used by later societies as a material resource to be worked with creating links with the past, often to legitimate claims to land and power. In contrast to this sense of deep past, we might recognise a generational sense of the past, with individuals directly linked to their immediate ancestors through well-developed notions of genealogy and descent. Genealogical thinking could provide an element of measured time; with real or invented events being connected to specific individuals recorded in genealogies. While, undoubtedly, many genealogies contained fictive elements, there was still an underlying notion of history and that events that happened in the past could impact on the present. Recording of ancestry, generation by generation, was undoubtedly a core way in which claims to power and land could be legitimated, and even relatively late, inauguration rituals could often include the public recitation of lineages. It has also been argued that the wider genealogical model of time can be seen in Eddic mythology, with each period seen as a link in a genealogical chain (Winterbourne 2004, 48-9).

These senses of chronology might also be recognised in the way in which social memory could be materialised, with different attitudes to time being expressed in the archaeological record in different ways. Not surprisingly, given the role of death in marking the succession of generations, cemeteries appear to form a key sphere in which conceptions of time might be made physical. In such contexts, the inherent disorder of the actual passage of generations (individuals die at various ages and in various circumstances) might be re-ordered to provide a more structured sense of genealogy (Sayer 2010). In some cases, such ordering may have impacted on features, such as the range of grave-goods deposited, that would be recognisable only during the celebration of the primary mortuary rituals (Devlin 2007, 19-41; Sayer 2010; Williams 2006, 36-78). In other contexts, generational relationships might be mapped, created and enhanced by 'repeated augmentation with graves and structural alteration' (Williams 2006, 13; see, e.g., Mizoguchi 1993; Kujit 2001). This strategy can be seen widely in some early medieval pre-Christian and conversion period burial traditions. Graves are often clustered into what are presumably family groups – such practices can be found widely across Anglo-Saxon England (e.g. Berinsfield, Oxfordshire (Boyle et al. 1995; Mill Hill, Deal (Parfitt and Brugman 1997)), while at Sutton Hoo groups of fifteen barrows of late sixth- and early seventh-century date are strung along a ridge above the River Deben (Carver 2005); this is almost certainly a dynastic burial ground, and despite difficulties in establishing a precise chronology for the graves, it appears that the cluster was initiated by a central line of cremation burials (Carver 2005, 311; Williams 2006, 158-62). On a monumental burial site such as this, social memory would have meant that the genealogical relationships of the deceased could be mapped and reconstructed on the ground.

These *chronotypes* should not be seen as oppositions, but as complementary ways of understanding the past – perceptions that might be equally valid for both Christians and pagans. Indeed, in past societies it might be quite possible for the two modes of thinking to operate together. For example, in thirteenth-century Norway rites for the inheritance of family estates required witnesses to 'count the ancestry back to the mound and heathen time' (Sundqvist 2002, 173; Zachrisson 1994). These implies both sense of time, a genealogical or generational sense of the past that can be mapped through counting family descent, and a sense of a deeper, internally undifferentiated past, in this case linked to a period before conversion. Crucially, while the generational past is expressed orally, the notion of the deeper past is symbolically represented through the presence of a burial mound. Other strategies to integrate the two conceptions of the past might also include the inclusion of divine figures into genealogies, such as the inclusion of gods in some Anglo-Saxon royal genealogies (Sisam 1953). Richard Bradley has also emphasised that in the re-use of prehistoric monuments could be punctuated by periods when there was no activity at the site. Despite the notion of continuity being invoked through secondary burial in barrows and similar activities, the link with the past was artificial and fictional; in such cases it might be seen as an attempt to reconcile a generational sense of the past with deeper notions of antiquity. Howard Williams has noted, for example, how in seventh-century Anglo-Saxon England, barrow burials were often deliberately sited in similar landscape positions to prehistoric Bronze Age round barrows (Williams 1999). The wider re-use of prehistoric monuments as the focus for cemeteries is well attested; often the cemeteries might also be subdivided into familial or household groups, meaning that such cemeteries might be invoking both a generational and a mythic sense of the past at one site. For example, at Mill Hill, Deal, the two clusters of burials are situated either side of a Bronze Age ring ditch (Parfitt and Brugman 1997), while at Harford Farm (Norfolk), two separate clusters of burials both focused on prehistoric burial mounds (Penn 2000).

Similar patterns can be seen outside Britain. At the cemetery at Bækkegård on Bornholm (Denmark) the burials were in three clusters of which only one focused on an earlier prehistoric cairn, while others were arranged further away. In this case, it seems that only one burial group benefited from the close association with a prehistoric monument (Thäte 2007, 222-3). A similar situation can be recognised at Over Hornbæk (Denmark), where a group of graves were located in directly relation to a megalithic barrow, while others were more widely spread in clusters to the south and east of the re-used monument (ibid., 223-4).

It is also regularly implicitly assumed that pagan religions had no sense of eschatology, with the assumption that they had no sense of prospective time and long-term destiny. A sense of an end of the profane world and some kind of final act of judgement also has clear wider connections to the notion of destiny and fate, which might in turn be influenced by behaviour in this world. Consequently, the denial to pagan societies of a sense of eschatology also implicitly denies pagan religions many of the other features implicit in the binary construction of paganism as lacking an ethical or world-rejecting notion. Despite the difficulties of trying to delineate pagan cosmography, it is certainly possible that some pagan societies had eschatological traditions. For example, the idea of *Ragnorok*, the final battle at the end of the world, is commonly found in Old Norse traditions, with some motifs found in skaldic stanza, and more fully set out in *Voluspá* (Hultgard 1991). While *Ragnorok* is admittedly only recorded in texts written after the conversion period, it is difficult to argue that the entire concept was a reaction to the Christian notion of final judgement. Although some individual motifs, such as the return of Baldr, may reflect a Christian influence, the wider narrative is distinctly different enough from the Domesday narrative to indicate a separate origin (for a similar methodological challenge see Hultkrantz 1980). While the possibility of avoiding *Ragnorok* may have been one motivation for conversion (Winterbourne 2004, 141), this entails the choice between competing eschatologies, rather than the first introduction of the underlying concept to a pagan milieu (for a different reading of this see North 2006). This is, of course, not to suggest that all pagan societies facing Christian conversion in the early medieval period had strongly developed senses of linear time and eschatological concepts; for example, it is likely that the seasonally nomadic Saami in Scandinavia used a different range of *chronotypes* than their Viking neighbours to the south (Bergman 2006). However, the dominance of cyclical notions of time and a lack of eschatology should be proved, rather than simply assumed, when modelling such pagan societies.

Finally, it is important to be aware of the complexity of even cyclical conceptions of time (witness the sheer size and scale of

4. Deconstructing paganism

Bronze and Neolithic monumentality which has a clear calendrical element). Bede wrote about the pagan Anglo-Saxon calendar, which consisted of twelve lunar months and the periodic addition of an extra month to keep pace with the solar cycle (Harrison 1976, 3-4). Effective use of such a calendar would require common agreement about when the additional months were to be inserted, and some form of measurement or monitoring of the passage of time. Like all calendars, it was of course cyclical, but the careful management required to ensure the correct measurement of time required a sense of progressive time for it to be effective.

Case study: death and time in the Iron Age East Baltic

It is possible to explore the varying notions of time held within pre-Christian societies by looking at a group of cemeteries from Late Iron Age Estonia. Saaremaa (also known as Ösel) which lies off the western coast of Estonia, is the second largest island in the Baltic after Gotland. It was one of the richest areas of Livonia. The archaeology of late Iron Age society on the island is well represented through the presence of a series of fortified power centres and harbours, as well as an extensive burial record (e.g. Mägi 2002, 2004). The island was drawn into the orbit of the Catholic church during the Northern Crusades and was conquered by the Sword Brothers in 1227 (Christiansen 1997). This leading to the spread of Christianity on the island, including the construction of a number of stone churches and chapels.

Although the arrival of the Church certainly led to developments in the burial rite, I want to focus here on burial customs in the 500 years before this event. Marika Mägi, in her overview of burial on the island, has identified four key phases in burial customs over this time (Mägi 2002, 137). The initial stage, beginning as early as the sixth century, saw significant re-use of prehistoric monuments as the site of cemeteries, including stone cairns and the distinctive rectangular *tarand*

87

graves. There was, though, little evidence for the construction of new monuments or markers over the graves themselves. The clear distinction in the earliest phase is the contrast between the placement of burials in association with earlier mortuary monuments, suggesting an interest in developing links with earlier ancestors, while at the same time there was far less interest in monumentalising individual graves. This may suggest less focus on 'fixing' the burials of individuals within the landscape. Ancestry appears thus to have been of importance when it intersected with a deep or mythic past, while more immediate genealogical relationships within the burial community were of lesser significance.

From the mid/late tenth century there appears to have been an increased use of stone circles and cairns over individual cremations. These can be seen clearly at sites such as Käku and Kurevere, where the cremation deposits were surrounded by stone kerbs, with some additional cremations being placed between the stone circles. Here we see the monumental fixing of the cremations acting as a visual mnemonic of the significance of individual identity, and potentially a renewed focus on kinship identities, invoking a stronger sense of the measurement of time as measured through the passing of generations. Conversely, there is a general decrease in the placement of cemeteries next to prehistoric monuments, the notable exception being the site of Piila, in central Saaremaa, which may have been re-using the site of a Bronze Age or pre-Roman Iron Age burial site (Mägi 2002, 43). Over the course of the eleventh century there is again a decline in visually fixing individual graves. The cremations at Kogula and Randvere are generally not marked, although a small number are still surrounded by stone circles. Despite the lack of individual markers, the cemeteries became more monumental overall, with a possible visual emphasis on corporate rather than personal identity. This is not to suggest that individual identities were not expressed in the burial rite, but it is clear that there is far less focus in the sphere of monumentality. We see generational/genealogical time being suppressed. In this period there is also little evidence for significant levels of monument re-use in the siting of cemeteries.

Finally, from the thirteenth century, broadly coinciding with the advent of Christianity, there is a major shift from cremation to inhumation. Apart from a few precocious inhumations of late twelfth-century date from the cemetery at Loona, the other inhumation cemeteries (Valjala, Karja and Viira) had no association with earlier burials, and no evidence for above-ground monumentalisation. Although found in the same general areas as previous Late Iron Age cremation cemeteries, there is no little evidence for the immediate juxtaposition of cremation and inhumation grounds. Instead, the evidence seems to suggest a clear break with earlier burial sites.

Even when sketched in broad strokes, as above, it can be seen that over the period from *c.* 600 to 1200 the materialisation and representation of time as recognisable through patterns of monumentalisation and re-use of earlier burial sites varied widely, shifting from a focus on the deep or mythic past in the seventh to ninth centuries, with little evidence for the expression of genealogy, to a greater focus on the burials of individuals from the tenth century onwards. This can be seen by the new emphasis on fixing individual graves through the construction of mounds and cairns, going hand-in-hand with a decrease in the re-use of earlier monuments. There was again a decline in the expression of individual identity in the mortuary rite from the eleventh century on – although there is little evidence for renewed use of prehistoric sites, the cemeteries themselves become monumentalised, but emphasising corporate rather than atomised identity. Finally, the advent of Christianity sees a key transition in mortuary rite (cremation to inhumation), and another shift in burial location away from the monumental eleventh-century sites and prehistoric sites, possibly marking a conceptual break from a 'pagan' past. If we were to explore these patterns of change in mortuary behaviour simply in terms of a 'pagan'/'Christian' model, we might be tempted to construct a simplistic model which emphasised a simple switch away from 'pagan' monuments to a new Christian landscape. However, by placing our understanding of the burial traditions into a longer-term perspective, we can see that conceptions of time were continually being reworked and reinterpreted within the half-millennium leading up to conversion, indeed even to within two hundred years of the advent of the Church. The notion of an essentialist 'pagan' notion of time in this context will simply not suffice. It is possible to further problematise the situation by a more detailed consideration of the evidence. For example, although most inhumation cemeteries have no relation to previous burial sites, there are hints from a few locations, such as Liiva, 1.5 km to the north-east of Viira, that inhumations may been close to a tenth-century cremation cemetery. Clearly, although it is possible to recognise broad tendencies, there were 'micro-traditions' reflecting very localised attitudes to the past, which could contrast even over an area of a few miles (cf. Lucy 2002).

Pagan perceptions of space

If the pagan sense of time can be problematised and demonstrated to be more complex than a simple opposition of 'cyclical time' versus 'linear time', then the same is also true of pre-Christian senses of space. It is clear that early medieval pagan landscapes were loaded with symbolic meaning (e.g. Semple 2002, 2010; Clay 2008). The inhabitants of non-Christian societies moved through a space inhabited by spirits, gods and ancestors. Natural places, rivers, lakes and prehistoric monuments were imbued with ritual significance; even at a more immediate scale, halls and settlements could be the site of a range of ritual practices and activities (e.g. Hamerow 2006; Walker 2010). The often implicit assumption, however, is that these sites were experienced only by those who lived within the locality. There have been relatively few attempts to impose an element of scale over this ritual landscapes. If we compare Christian senses of ritual landscapes, then it is immediately clear that symbolic space operated in a nested level of scales, ranging from the immediate ideological construction of micro-

4. Deconstructing paganism

spaces with the church or home, to the symbolic geography of the parish, mapped through wayside crosses, holy wells and the ritual procession of the parish bounds at Rogationtide, to the wider regional geography of cathedrals and regional pilgrimage sites, proceeding at a larger scale to routes of international pilgrimage (Santiago; Rome) and to a wider cosmological mapping of space placing Jerusalem at the centre of the known world (O'Sullivan 2001). There have been relatively few attempts to explore this sense of graduated ritual landscape in a pagan context. It has been suggested that in Anglo-Saxon England there was a correlation between hundred meeting places and possible temples (Meaney 1995, 37). It is certainly possible that there may be have been a coincidence of religious sites of greater than local significance with important secular power centres; for example, the range of unusual structures at the Anglian palace at Yeavering and the fact that it was the site of a key episode in the conversion of the Anglian kings of Northumbria may imply that site had an important religious meaning, as well as a secular one (*HE* II.14). The same applies to the pagan temple at Goodmanham (East Yorkshire) recorded by Bede as being destroyed by Coifi, the newly converted former chief-priest of King Edwin of Northumbria (*HE* II.13). These suggest that there was a hierarchy of holy sites that broadly parallels the secular hierarchy. On a broad North European scale it is certainly possible to recognise a close correspondence between areas of major ritual activity and centres of social and political power. The major foci of cult activity at sites such as Uppåkra (Sweden), Tissø (Denmark) Borg (Lofoten, Norway) and Uppsala were clearly connected to major local power centres (Larsson and Lentorp 2004; Jørgensen 2003; Munch et al. 2003; Nielsen 1997). This homology between sites of secular and ritual importance need not surprise us; however, it is important to consider the possibility of alternative ritual landscapes that crossed and transcended political boundaries. If one approaches this topic in the *longue durée* then it is certainly possible to recognise the presence of religious cosmologies being mapped out in a very large, indeed international, scale.

This can be seen clearly in recent work on Stonehenge (Wilt-shire) and its surrounding landscape. The Neolithic and Bronze Age henge complex and its hinterland were undoubt-edly an area of very high symbolic density, however, its cosmological import went well beyond its immediate locality and even its regional location in the chalklands of Wessex. The bluestone circle at the heart of the monument was constructed with stone taken from south-west Wales, over 150 miles dis-tant. As well as drawing symbolically important resources from a long distance away, it is clear that Stonehenge itself drew in people from well beyond its own regional context, with isotope analysis on graves in the immediate vicinity indicating that some individuals buried there had journeyed at least 150 miles, and possibly even from the Continent. The so-called 'Amesbury archer', an early Bronze Age burial found just three miles away from Stonehenge, may have come from Central Europe and the so-called 'Boy with the amber necklace' may even have come from the Mediterranean (Evans et al. 2006; Wessex Archaeo-logy 2008; RGS 2010). The symbolic importance of using stone taken from a particular distant source, found at Stonehenge, can also be paralleled in a different way elsewhere in prehis-toric Britain by the evidence for the special preference given to the use of stone taken from remote quarries at Scafell Pike, high in the Lake District, for making stone hand-axes (Bradley and Edmonds 1993). Even from these two examples, it is clear that the religious landscapes of Neolithic and Bronze Age Brit-ain had distant horizons. The ritual significance of landscapes could transcend their immediate localities and make links with distant locations. Equally, for individuals, sites of ritual impor-tance could be located well away from their immediate environment, and might cause them to travel significant dis-tances. Even for those who did not make the journey, knowledge and understanding of sites such as Stonehenge are likely to have been geographically widespread. In this context, to talk of society being limited to a microcosmic world view is clearly wrong.

A second example of the international scale of pre-Christian religion confirms the extent to which ritual landscapes could operate on a very large scale. While there is much that is misunderstood about late Iron Age druidism in Western Europe, it is clear that it also acted on a large stage (Chadwick 1966; Green 1992). Julius Caesar refers to periodic meetings of druids at 'a consecrated place in the territories of the Carnutes, which is reckoned the central region of the whole of Gaul' (*Gallic Wars* 6.13). This seems to indicate some level of organisation for religious ritual beyond the tribal, and possibly implies a wider symbolic geography of Gaul, with Carnutes identified as a pan-tribal centre of ritual significance. Caesar also refers to the belief that druidism originated in Britain; whether actually true or not, this belief indicated a sense that Gallic religious practices and their associated mythology had a cognitive map that operated in some way on an international level.

Further evidence for the potential international scale of late Iron Age cosmographies can be found in Anglesey (Wales). While the popular association of Anglesey with druidism appears to come from an over-optimistic reading of Tacitus' *Annals* (Book XIV), the island was the site of a major ritualised deposition of metalwork in the lake at Llyn Cerrig Bach. Some of this metalwork had clearly been imported from beyond the immediate region, including southern England and Ireland (Macdonald 2007, 152-7). This is not the only evidence of possible unusual external features indicative of possible long-distance communication in Anglesey. Two stone pillars from Trefollwyn, one carved, are unique to Britain, but appear to have been part of a tradition of La Tène carved stone pillars that spreads from the Rhineland, Brittany and Ireland (Edwards 1998); this is again suggestive of long-distance religious links across Iron Age Europe. This evidence is strongly supportive of an Iron Age religious cosmology that could articulate long-distance travel and movement of people and objects. Certainly, by the Roman period major shrines, such as Bath and *Fontes Sequanae* in Burgundy at the source of the River Seine, were attracting pilgrims from across the empire (Green 1999).

If we are able to identify religious practices with a clear macrocosmic aspect in late Iron Age Europe and the Roman empire, then such connections could have operated in the same area in the early medieval period. In some cases these are recorded only in documentary sources. Henry of Livonia records that priests carrying out conversions in central Livonia destroyed a temple and grove that was believed to have been the birthplace of Tharapita, a major god of the people of Saaremaa, which lies off the Estonian coast (*Chronicle of Henry of Livonia* 24.5). Other possible cases may be distinguished through the archaeological evidence. For example, excavation has shown continued activity within the inner precinct at the internationally important Roman cult centre at Bath well into the fifth century and possibly the sixth (Cunliffe and Davenport 1985, 74-5). The recovery of at least one early medieval penannular brooch from the spring itself also suggests continued cult activity at a site which at its height attracted pilgrims from across the Roman empire (Youngs 1995). While it is probable that votive activity at the site lost its international dimension from the fifth century onwards, the site appears to have continued to have a high profile in the Anglo-Saxon mind, as it is almost certainly the place described in the eighth-century Old English poem *The Ruin*.

Even where there is no direct evidence for cult activity, it is clear that certain sites loomed large in ritual memory during the early medieval period. The stretch of the River Witham south of Lincoln was a major focus of ritual deposition during the Iron Age and the Roman period. The scale of activity (along a stretch at least 10 km long) would suggest a ritual significance for the river above and beyond the immediately local communities. While there is no direct evidence for votive deposition continuing along this stretch during the early Anglo-Saxon period, such practices appear to have re-emerged in the middle to late Anglo-Saxon period and during the post-Conquest period, when a series of monasteries were founded in the area, and numerous medieval objects, including swords, were placed in the river (Stocker and Everson 2003; Lund 2010). Despite the temporary cessation of deposition during the fifth to seventh centuries, it is clear that there was a continued

4. Deconstructing paganism

memory of the ritual symbolism which enabled the tradition to be revived at a later date.

Sarah Semple has also highlighted the evidence of the continued ritual importance of key places in the landscape being recognised in the Anglo-Saxon period in her recent re-analysis of so-called *hearg* (OE *hearg* = 'temple') sites in southern England (Semple 2007). She has shown that such sites were often a focus of religious activity in the prehistoric and Roman periods; despite there being little evidence of overt cultic activity in the fifth to seventh centuries, the use of the *hearg* place-name suggests their ritual importance continued to resonate in this period. In some cases, these *hearg* sites occupied dominant landscape positions, which were visible from far beyond the immediate surrounding area. It is likely that such sites must have fitted into a wider cosmological landscape, and were not simply important at a simply local level. It is clear that dominant features in the landscape could also be imbued with a ritual significance in this period, and again these are likely to have had an importance on a wider regional or even national scale. For example, a number of mountains in Poland, such as Lysa Góra and Mount Ślęza, appear to have been significant pre-Christian cult centres (Buko 2008, 108-17). Each is the site of unusual stone sculptures and has produced evidence of possible cult activity, and the latter was recorded as being a site of particular veneration by Thietmar of Merseburg (*Chronicon* 6.59). There may also be alternative ways of exploring long-distance ritual contacts. For example, work on Anglo-Saxon cremation urns has demonstrated that urns from cemeteries a considerable distance apart (e.g. Sancton, East Yorkshire; Baston, south-west Lincolnshire) were decorated with impressions made with the same dies, although the clay used was local (Arnold 1983). This raises the intriguing possibility of peripatetic potters specialising in creating pottery vessels with a primary ritual purpose. The distances involved would appear to cut across localised family or extended kinship groups and indicate at least some sense of commonality in the expression of specific ritualised acts over considerable distances.

Conclusion

This chapter has attempted to address some of the pervading conceptions about pagan or pre-/non-Christian religion in early medieval Europe, which are as equally enduring and influential as existing perceptions of Christiianity. However, whereas essentialist models of Christianity are being increasingly critiqued, attitudes to paganism have been explored less thoroughly. While researchers working on prehistoric material may well be producing increasingly subtle readings of ritual behaviour, these understandings often do not reach those working on early Christianity, who instead have turned to anthropology and ethnography as a source for understanding the societies which were confronted by the early Christian missionaries. However, it might be argued that this recourse to anthropological parallels and injudicious use of analogy is actually consolidating existing stereotypes of non-Christian religious belief; it has been shown that notions of microcosmic and macrocosmic religions which may be of some limited application in the context of understanding the impact of globalisation and colonialism on religious practices in nineteenth- and twentieth-century Africa are not appropriate for understanding religious change in early medieval Europe. The danger with these essentialist models of pagan religious practice that depict pre-Christian ritual worlds as fundamentally microcosmic with limited spatial and temporal boundaries, is that it underplays the potential diversity and variation within them. There is no scope for acknowledging that pagan practice can vary across space or, perhaps, more importantly, over time. This lack of acknowledgement of the capacity of pagan practices to change and evolve ultimately results in a denial of agency. Pagans are seem as incapable of acting creatively within their own world view, with the only release from a cosmological and historical stasis being achieved by the external invocation of Christianity.

5

Religions in contact

The previous four chapters, rather than engaging in a close analysis of the detailed process of religious change in the early medieval period, have instead tried to explore some of the wider conceptual issues related to this topic. It has been suggested that the meta-narratives linked to the spread of Christianity have been dominated by one of 'Constantinian' conversion, which sees the adoption of Christianity as primarily an act of *realpolitik* led from the top. There has been far less consideration of the more drawn-out process of adoption of the new religion by the non-élite portions of the population. Both archaeologists and historians have recognised the varying ways in which local expressions or modes of Christianity could be recognised across Europe, whether understood as Peter Brown's 'micro-Christendoms' or Martin Carver's 'intellectual communities'. It has been argued, though, that these fail to reflect the varying ways in which Christianity might be adopted within, rather than between societies. The dominance of research on monumentality and high-status sites by archaeologists working on early medieval material has perpetuated the emphasis on the role of élite in the conversion process.

The argument then moved to a consideration of the way in which archaeologists have engaged with the study of religion and ritual, arguing that the study of religion in the first millennium AD has been primarily structured on a series of key binary oppositions that contrast pagan societies with Christianity in a range of ways that has meant that the approaches to the study of these religious beliefs have gone down very different paths. Work on pre-Christian religious belief has been essentially an archaeological project, whereas the study of early Christianity has been fundamentally historical in outlook. I have argued, drawing on notions of structure and agency, that a more unified approach to the consideration of Christianity and pagan belief systems might transcend these conceptual divides. I also suggested that an 'identity approach' to the study of early medieval religion might prove useful, allowing a focus on the context of religious expression and emphasising the need to map the spread of Christianity not simply spatially, but through its colonisation of fields of discourse within a given society.

Moving on to a more detailed exploration of the role of texts and literacy in the construction of the early medieval Church, I have attempted to emphasise the importance of non-textual sources of authority in the practice and transmission of Christianity, arguing that a renewed focus on materiality allows archaeology to resume a more central place in the exploration of the conversion process. Finally, in Chapter 4, I moved from the dominant metaphors that characterise the perception of Christianity to a consideration of the key tropes that have dominated how early medieval pagan beliefs have been characterised. I suggested that there has been a tendency, ultimately derived from over simplistic borrowings from anthropology, to model pagan societies as being caught in a temporal and spatial microcosm in contrast to the macrocosmic scope of Christianity. Instead, I would contend, early medieval societies could be far more complex, and their belief systems could encompass complex and contrasting models of time and space. As a consequence, any models of Christian and pagan encounter that are predicated on a simple micro- versus macro-cosmic model fail to do justice to the complexity of this engagement. In this final chapter I want to try to take some of these theoretical ideas and apply them to some practical case studies in an attempt to see how an application of some of the concepts developed in previous chapters might be translated into the practice.

5. Religions in contact

Converting Anglo-Saxon England, 600-700

The major cemetery at Sutton Hoo (Suffolk), with its extravagant grave-goods and elaborate monumentality, has iconic status in the study of middle Anglo-Saxon society (Carver 1998a, 2005; Evans 1986). With its most lavish burial, the early seventh-century boat burial in Mound 1, occurring within a generation of the arrival of the Gregorian mission to convert the Anglo-Saxon kingdoms, it has not surprisingly become a site that has been used repeatedly to explore the nature of burial rites in this crucial period, which saw not just the rise of Christianity, but also the consolidation the Anglo-Saxon kingdoms that dominated the political landscape of England until the advent of the Vikings in the ninth century.

Religion, both pagan and Christian, has long taken a central role in interpreting the burials at Sutton Hoo, with arguments being advanced for both a 'Christian' and a 'pagan' identity for some of the graves (particularly Mound 1). Proponents of a Christian identity point to the Christian nature of some of the grave goods, such as the Byzantine material, including the silver spoons and plate (Webster and Backhouse 1991, 16). Alternatively, it has been suggested that Mound 1 marks an instance of 'defiant paganism'; an ostentatious and deliberate attempt to use burial rites to signal an affiliation with the North Sea and Scandinavian world, in distinction to the Christian, Frankish and even ultimately Byzantine identities being cultivated by kings of Kent (Carver 2005, 313). It could even be argued that the Mound 1 burial was a deliberately syncretic event, drawing on both pagan and Christian material vocabularies. This latter point of view brings to mind Bede's records of Raedwald's positioning of a Christian altar next to a pagan altar (*HE* II15); the regular identification of Sutton Hoo as the burial ground of Raedwald and his dynasty meaning that even if he was not the person placed in Mound 1, he may have been closely implicated in its construction. Whichever argument is supported, it is predicated on identifying religious affiliation in a relatively simplistic way onto the burial rite: boat burial, monumental mound building, military equipment as burial goods being seen as fundamentally pagan and Scandinavian, whereas inhumation, gold and garnet jewellery and Byzantine plate are seen as essentially Kentish and Christian. The overall religious content of the burial is seen as a function of the relative weight or significance placed on the components of the mortuary ritual. However, underlying this discourse is the fundamental assumption that burial rites were ultimately related to religious affiliation. This might, however, be disputed, although it is important to emphasise that querying the role of 'religion' in the burial rite need not automatically mean a retreat into an overly simplistic socio-economic interpretative paradigm, which avoids exploring questions of meaning or identity. Burial traditions in this period are clearly closely tied into issues of personal and social identity. The real question is, then, which identities are being expressed or repressed in these burials, and how are these being read?

It has been suggested earlier (with an example from the Life of St Martin of Tours) that burial was not automatically seen as a domain in which religious affiliation was overtly expressed. Obviously there are about 200 years and 500 miles between St Martin and the body in Mound 1. However, this should make us start asking questions. It is salutary to look at some of the documentary evidence connected to Christian mission in the Anglo-Saxon world and its attitude to burial. According to the material in Bede, Augustine is interested in how to deal with pagan temples and holy sites, but does not address the issue of burial at all (e.g. *HE* I.30). The issue of burial is also noticeably lacking in the Letters of St Boniface, although he challenges a range of practices (sacrifices; 'idol worship') which he clearly identifies as 'pagan' (e.g. *Letters* XXIX). Elsewhere on the Continent attempts to enforce some degree of uniformity over burial only develop in the later eighth century, including Charlemagne's attempt to prevent cremation and the use of burial mounds among the newly conquered Saxons – even in this case it is clear that this policy was as much about suppressing

Saxon ethnic identity as enforcing Christian dogma (Effros 1997). On a more European scale, the crystallisation of the liturgy connected to death and dying only really occurred in the eighth and ninth centuries, primarily through the influence of the Carolingian rulers who disseminated new attitudes to the ritualisation of death initially developed in Ireland and only reaching the Anglo-Saxon and Carolingian church in the eighth century. It was only with such centralising tendencies that the Church showed increased interest in direct control over the mortuary rituals themselves (Paxton 1990).

This all suggests that on the Christian side of the equation (or at least from the perspective of the Christian clergy), burial was not seen as a sphere of particular relevance to religious belief and practice. Does the same hold true for the pre-Christian Anglo-Saxons? It is harder to be definitive, but it is useful to look at the range of identities that are clearly expressed in their burial rites. A series of studies in recent years have demonstrated that there are certain underlying structural principles that appear to influence variability in the early Anglo-Saxon burial rite, and presumably the range of social identities which are being expressed. The two key axes of variability appear to be familial identity (as broadly defined to include gender and age, which would have affected the position of individuals within kin groups) and status (as broadly defined in terms of economic, social and personal power). These basic axes appear to be expressed both through grave-goods and burial monumentality. While there is much localised variability in the precise ways in which these variations are expressed between individual cemeteries (Lucy 2002), these basic underlying principles appear to be found across much of early medieval European burial traditions during the middle centuries of the first millennium AD (Halsall 1995). Rather than religious identity being the prime variable in Anglo-Saxon burial rites, other identities are instead being foregrounded, identities that arguably have more day-to-day relevance in their lives.

It is crucial, though, to appreciate that this argument is not intended to suggest that there was no religious aspect or dimension to burial rites at all. Doubtless, Christian prayers were said over the graves of dead Christians, and the placement of grave-goods among pagans explained in terms of local mythologies and eschatologies. Rather, the relationship between the form and context of the burial rite was only very loosely conceived; there was no clearly formulated relationship between belief and burial practice, with religious identity being latent and submerged rather than clearly articulated through mortuary ritual. To argue over the 'religious identity' of Sutton Hoo is ultimately to ask the wrong question. We should not be asking 'What is the religious identity of this burial?' but rather 'How did burial come to be seen as an appropriate sphere for the expression of religious belief?'.

If one analyses the burial goods within Mound 1 at Sutton Hoo, the real interest is not in trying to establish which 'cultural package' (Frankish or Scandinavian) is in the ascendant, but rather in addressing the fact they are juxtaposed. Similar questions might be asked about other important burials of this period, such as the burial at Prittlewell (Essex), where mound burial, Scandinavian style buckets and a lyre are juxtaposed with the placement of gold foil crosses within the grave, Kentish style buckles, a Coptic bowl and a Byzantine silver spoon (MOLAS 2004). As Carver has rightly argued with reference to Sutton Hoo, 'the references are not specific, as in "pagan" or "Christian" or a "Roman Emperor" but allusive and the result may be described as a "palimpsest" of allusions' (Carver 2005, 312). It is not necessary to set up the interpretation of such graves in oppositional religious terms, as either 'Christian' or 'pagan' either overtly, or entwined and embedded with associated ethnic identities or alignments (e.g. Scandinavian; Frankish). While the tensions between the Anglian and Kentish kingdoms was undoubtedly significant, it is important to remember that it is highly unlikely that the burial rites at Sutton Hoo or Prittlewell would have been viewed by individuals from Kent. Instead, these rites are more likely to have been aimed primarily at internal audiences within the kingdom, even within the ruling dynasty. In such contexts, it is unlikely that expressions of religious identity were the primary message.

As Carver has quite rightly emphasised, ship-burial was an entirely new introduction into Britain. This is not a typically Anglo-Saxon burial rite; while there are certainly elements of the burial rite that have links to past mortuary traditions in eastern England, the most notable feature of the wide range of burial rites used is their novelty. We do not see at this site an expression of ultra-traditionalism in the face of Christian innovation in burial rites. Indeed, at Sutton Hoo there is a progressive rejection of cremation, a rite that might be seen as most distinctively Anglian. If, for the sake of argument, we accept Carver's argument that the Sutton Hoo burials represent 'defiant paganism' then we are not seeing a promotion of an indigenous ritual belief system as antithetical to Christianity, but rather a construction or creation of a 'third way', a reaction against both Christianity and local Anglian ritual practices. This break with local traditions is also made manifest in the indication that Sutton Hoo is a new cemetery showing a move away from an earlier 'folk cemetery' perhaps in the later sixth century. Elsewhere, at Snape (Suffolk), although the cemetery falls out of use in the later sixth century, there is a clear distinction between the relatively traditional cremations used during the earlier phase of the cemetery's life and the later period of experimentation and novelty associated with the later graves, particularly the transition to inhumation and boat burials (Filmer-Sankey and Pestell 2000).

This is important, as it suggests that the desire for new forms of funerary rites come before the advent of Augustine in Kent. Rather than seeing Mound 1 at Sutton Hoo as a 'pagan' reaction to the advent of Christianity to the south of the Thames, it is possible to take a slightly more long-term perspective and see the search for new and novel ways of expressing identity through burial in East Anglia and the adoption of Christianity by Aethelbert in Kent as alternative and parallel strategies in the face of a range of other social processes at this time, a period which saw evidence for increasingly permanent levels of social and economic ranking (Arnold 1988; Scull 1992, 1993; Yorke 1990). This increased stratification allowed, and indeed required, the élites to develop new ways of ideologically marking and consolidating their social position. Significantly, this approach restores a level of agency to the Anglian élite; they are not simply reactive in the face of Christianity, but show the ability to act as ideological impresarios, using innovation within the field of ritual (in the widest sense of the word) as a way of constructing new identities.

This discussion has suggested that we should stop using Sutton Hoo as a lens for looking at Christianity or the pagan reaction to it. Instead, I have suggested that the issue of a defined 'religious' identity was simply never on the agenda. Snape, Prittlewell and Sutton Hoo were not primarily attempts by pagan kings to send a message about religious identity in the face of a rising tide of Christianity. They are certainly about identity politics, but not specifically religious identity. Instead, the key message is fundamentally about the establishment of new discourses about power, rank and status within their social milieu. There appears to have been a clear aim to create a new material vocabulary connected to wealth and status, distinguishing the élite from the wider population. This marks a clear departure from the ranked, but more fluid, organisation of Anglo-Saxon society before the late sixth century, where status was more likely to be essentially expressed within rather than between social units (Scull 1993, 72-5). Hierarchies of power were likely to be relatively flat, with the household as the focus of social organisation (Woolf 1997). Instead, the later sixth century onwards was a period when there was more permanent social ranking, with the development of a clear group of élite families, distinct from the wider population. It is in this context that the East Anglian and Kentish developments need to be placed; we are seeing innovation to consolidate and distinguish new élites from other groups within society. This was done using a series of strategies, including spatial separation and innovation in burial rites. We might also add the adoption of new forms of dress, such as the use of gold and garnet jewellery, and Style II decoration (Høilund Nielsen 1999).

So far, this narrative, although questioning the religious underpinnings of some of the debates around Sutton Hoo, has in many ways continued some of the traditional discourses about power and identity. Most obviously, although critiquing existing interpretations, it has still been focused on 'classic' sites connected to the very highest ranks of Anglo-Saxon society. It has also, in some senses, worked within other traditional paradigms. In the early seventh century, 'pagan' East Anglia and 'Christian' Kent both appear to be 'intellectual communities' which can be spatially mapped, although it has been suggested that changes in the burial rite in East Anglia might be seen as parallel with, rather than in reaction to, the adoption of Christianity in Kent. However, I argued earlier in this book that while the notions of 'intellectual communities' or 'micro-Christendoms' are a powerful way of looking at the spread of Christianity, they focus on looking at difference in the way in which the Church was adopted and expressed *between* communities. It is also important to look at different modes of engagement with Christianity *within* communities.

Anglo-Saxon England:
conversion and gender

I want to now carry this exploration of Anglo-Saxon conversion forward and try to take an alternative view of developments in the burial rite in the middle and late seventh century. However, in this case I want to introduce a new dimension of analysis, that of gender. The expression of gendered identities in the Anglo-Saxon burial rites over the course of the seventh century goes through major changes. This can be seen most clearly if one considers élite burials. It is noticeable that the extravagant élite burials of the early seventh century are almost uniformly male in nature. The wealthy graves at Snape, Prittlewell, Sutton Hoo, Taplow (Berks), Broomfield (Essex) and Caenby (Lincs) are all predominantly male (Filmer-

Sankey and Pestell 2000; MOLAS 2004; Carver 2005; Burgess 1886, 331-5; Smith 1902, 320-6; Leahy 2007, 93-6). Although in some cases, such as at Snape and Sutton Hoo, there are females interred within the cemetery, their mortuary rituals appear far less extravagant. However, by the mid-seventh century this balance is being reversed. Instead, there is a significant rise in wealthy female burials, including Swallowcliffe Down, Roundway Down (Wiltshire), Desborough (Northamptonshire), Street House (Yorkshire), Westfield Farm, Ely (Cambridgeshire) (Speake 1989; Meaney 1964, 274; Lucy et al. 2009a; Sherlock and Simmons 2008; Lucy et al. 2009b). We can see an emphasis on female gender being expressed in a number of ways at this site. Most obvious is the investment in grave-goods, both in absolute terms, such as the set of gold and garnet jewellery found accompanying Grave 42 at Street House or the gold and silver necklace and two complete glass palm cups found with Grave 1 at Westfield Farm, Ely (Sherlock and Simmons 2008; Lucy 2009b, 88). However, female burials could also stand out through a central placing within the cemetery, as at Street House where Grave 42 was surrounded by an unusual placement of burials in a rectangle surrounding it, or Westfield Farm, Ely, where Grave 1 may have been under a barrow (Lucy 2009b, 84). Isolated élite burials could also be marked by barrows, such as at Swallowcliffe Down and Roundway Down (Speake 1989; Meaney 1964, 273-4).

These kind of distinctions can be recognised not only among the highest level of cemeteries. At Bloodmoor Hill (Suffolk), the mid- to late seventh-century cemetery produced a series of wealthy female graves but no particularly wealthy male graves; the authors commented that it 'is unusual that the main axis of distinction should lie so strongly between furnished/gendered female burial and all other groups' (Lucy et al. 2009a, 422-3). Even the more distinguished male burials of later seventh-century date, such as Lowbury Hill (Berkshire) are not particularly wealthy in terms of items deposited within the grave (Geake 2002, 147-8; Fulford and Rippon 1994).

We have a number of alternative models that might explain

this gender disparity. It might be that high-status males are being buried in the same locations as high-status females, but their graves are not strongly marked out or distinguished through the deposition of elaborate grave-goods and furnishings. It may be that some of the graves lacking significant quantities of grave-goods at sites such as Bloodmoor Hill are of as high status as the more wealthy female graves. A more likely alternative is that high-status males and high-status females are being buried in spatially distinct locations. It is noticeable that there is good evidence that 'final phase' cemeteries often appear to be contemporary to nearby ecclesiastical sites, suggesting that there is some element of choice in where individuals are being interred – the cemetery with its wealthy female central burial at Westfield Farm, Ely, appears to have been in use in the early years of the double-house founded on the Isle of Ely by Etheldreda in 673 (Lucy et al. 2009b), while early burials in Old Minster at Winchester overlapped with the latest burials at Winnall Down II (Geake 2002, 151). In both cases the two cemeteries were under a mile apart. Over a slightly longer distance, the cemetery at Street House, Redcar, appears to have been developed well after the foundation of the monastic houses at Hartlepool and Whitby, which are both within about 15 miles (Sherlock and Simmons 2008); Geake has also drawn attention to the appearance of a series of wealthy mound burials taking place in the Peak District after the establishment of the monastery at Repton (Derbyshire) (Geake 2002, 152; 1997, 149). In the last quarter of the seventh century churches appear to have become increasingly used as dynastic burial grounds by members of major royal lines, such as those of Kent and Northumbria, as well as members of dynasties linked to smaller sub-kingdoms (Blair 2005, 229). We thus have the potential to distinguish between two different strategies for burial among seventh-century élites; high-status men often opting for burial at ecclesiastical sites, while women of a similar position are being placed in wealthy cemeteries beyond the bounds of church establishments.

It is possible that we see here a distinction between pagan

women and Christian men, with females maintaining more traditional burial rites. This is not altogether unlikely; it has been noted that within Anglo-Saxon ruling dynasties, even well into the seventh century, numerous individuals might remain unbaptised, potentially out of a pragmatic decision to back both Christian and pagan horses (Yorke 2003, 245). Women clearly had a tradition of having considerable agency within the religious and ritual realm within the pagan Anglo-Saxon world, and it is not impossible that they continued to exercise this autonomy with reference to the process of conversion. However, many of the high-status female burials contain objects which appear to have explicit Christian connotations; for example, cross-shaped pendants have been recovered from a series of graves, including Desborough (Northamptonshire), White Low (Derbyshire), Lechlade (Gloucestershire) and Bloodmoor Hill (Suffolk) (see Crawford 2004, 92). Other Christian objects include the liturgical sprinkler of western British manufacture from Swallowcliffe Down (Wiltshire), a burial that also contained a silver spoon and a satchel decorated with cross-decorated mounts (Speake 1989). More realistically we appear to have a distinction between élite Christian males being largely buried at ecclesiastical sites, while élite Christian women are being largely buried outside such church centres. There are several records of Anglo-Saxon kings taking ecclesiastical orders before their deaths, and one basis for this distinction may be between the burial of those who have taken holy orders and those (mainly women) who have not (Yorke 2005). However, the close juxtaposition of the Westfield Farm cemetery to the convent at Ely may imply that even women who had taken the decision to become nuns may be adopting different burial rites to their male companions. Do we thus see a situation where the distinction in the burial rite is not structured on the basis of a distinction between 'pagan' and 'Christian' or even 'ecclesiastical' and 'secular', but 'male' and 'female'? We have here differing responses to the advent of Christianity being mapped spatially, not as mutually distinct 'intellectual communities' but as complimentary strategies within the same socio-cultural milieu.

It is possible to explore these gender based response to Christian burial further by considering some examples in which alternative gender balances can be recognised. These include a number of burials from the developing *wics* (trading sites) in Anglo-Saxon England. At the Buttermarket Cemetery, Ipswich (Suffolk) there was a higher proportion of masculine to feminine assemblages indentified – the reverse of the general pattern known elsewhere (e.g. Harford Farm or Bloodmoor Hill) (Scull 2010, 281), with several male burials including weapons, including Grave 1306 which was accompanied by a seax, two spears, a shield, two glass palm cups, and a buckle and belt fittings (ibid., 139-40). At Southampton (*Hamwic*), the seventh-century inhumation burials from the St Mary's Stadium site also included a number of richly furnished male burials, such as Grave 5537, which was accompanied by a sword, a seax, a shield, two spearheads and a knife and buckle, another grave (5537) contained a seax, a shield and two spearheads; there was also an unusual double burial with each occupant provided with a seax, one with a scabbard and belt-suite (Birbeck et al. 2005, 27-46). The presence of distinct high-status male burials at such incipient central places is exciting. It appears to suggest that these settlements may have offered those operating within them the literal and symbolic space to express status in death in ways that might not have been open to them elsewhere. One possible explanation for this is that these are individuals who have access to wealth generated through trade and exchange, but are not necessarily embedded within the increasingly stratified webs of dynastic and kinship relations that were the pre-requisite of gaining access to ecclesiastical burial grounds. They were not able to gain entry to the new symbolic domains being developed within the context of ecclesiastical space, but could find room for manoeuvre within the developing power relations being structured within the nascent trading sites of Middle Anglo-Saxon England.

Anglo-Saxon England: revealing and concealing belief

The wealthy seventh-century female burials provide a useful way into looking at other ways that belief and other identities were revealed and concealed in the conversion period in Anglo-Saxon England. It has already been noted that the seventh century in many ways appears to mark a rupture in burial rites, with the adoption of a new and reduced repertoire of grave-goods, changes in the representation of gender and often a physical dislocation of cemetery location. However, I want now to try to draw out some threads of continuity that can be found in the wealthy female graves of this period.

A number of classes of personal items were associated with fifth-/sixth-century female burials in Anglo-Saxon England. Most obvious are dress items, the range of brooches, beads, and wrist clasps that adorned female clothing (Lucy 2000, 25-48). A second type of grave-goods are the more functional items, such as weaving battens and other textile working tools, keys, knives and chatelaines (ibid.); these may also have had a wider symbolic function as a mark of female gender. Finally, there are also items which may have had some kind of amuletic or apotropaic purpose, including fossils, Roman coins and brooches and a range of other idiosyncratic items (Meaney 1981).

The change in burial traditions in the seventh century certainly appears to have included a shift in the range of dress items being placed within graves, presumably reflecting a wider alteration in female clothing in this period. There is a clear movement from brooches and long strings of beads to pins and necklaces of monochrome beads and sometimes pendants (Geake 1992). As noted above, these pendants often carry explicit Christian imagery, almost always a cross symbol. However, while there is a change in objects used as dress items, there is a wider continuity in the other classes of items included with graves. Chatelaines, knives, latch-lifters and items related to textile production continue to be placed in graves and the deposition of items that might be interpreted as amuletic or propitiatory may even have increased slightly (Meaney 1981).

While there may be a broad continuity in the placement of functional items and amulets within seventh-century female graves, what is more interesting is the way in which they are physically deployed within the grave itself. Rather than always being placed on or next to the corpse in an open manner, there is increasing evidence for the containment of non-dress items within graves, with objects being increasingly placed in bags and caskets. Examples of grave-goods in wooden caskets include Grave 15 at Bloodmoor Hill (Suffolk), where a comb, a shell and an iron ring with beads and pendants attached to it were placed in a casket (Lucy et al. 2009a, 395). The casket itself was placed within the wooden coffin. A more elaborate example of the use of caskets to contain grave-goods is the bed burial from Swallowcliffe Down, where a wooden casket at the left foot of the body contained a liturgical sprinkler, a silver spoon, five silver safety pins, a strap mount, two beads, two knives and a bone comb, while near the right foot was placed a leather satchel decorated with elaborate mounts (Speake 1989, 24-80). At Boss Hall, Ipswich, the woman buried in Grave 93 was accompanied by a wooden box containing a composite disc brooch, a set of silver cosmetic items and a necklace with gold and silver pendants (Scull 2009, 17-18). Less spectacular examples include Grave 14 from Butler's Field, Lechlade (Gloucestershire), where a wooden box at the foot of the body contained a 'threadbox', a pair of iron shears, a cowrie shell and a fragment of a bead (Boyle et al. 1998, 58-9). Grave-goods were not only being concealed in wooden boxes and caskets. There is also evidence for the placement of a similar range of items within organic bags of cloth or leather. At Bloodmoor Hill, the chatelaine complexes from Graves 11 and 23 were both seemingly swathed or wrapped in textile (Lucy et al. 2009a, 391-3, 401), while at Harford Farm (Norfolk), the body placed in Grave 33 was accompanied by a textile bag containing a necklace, toilet set and chatelaine (Penn 2000, 31-4). Given the generally poor preservation of organic remains in graves, it is likely that the number of objects being placed within bags is under-represented in the archaeological record – in some cases the actual position of the body indicates that articles were concealed. For example, in a grave from Eton Rowing Lake (Berks) and a burial from Orsett (Essex) the body was placed on top of a collection of amuletic items (Boyle et al. 2002, 31-3; Webster 1985).

This tension between concealment and display has been noted before and begins to problematise the relationship between the body and grave-goods (Williams 2006, 75-7; 2010). Taking a slightly different approach, Sally Crawford has argued that items not directly associated with the body in these graves should be interpreted as 'votive' offerings (Crawford 2004). In these graves we see certainly see one of the key changes in the seventh century as not the end of placement of items indicative of symbolic gender roles and possessing amuletic functions in graves, but rather an increasing disassociation from the corpse itself. It seems to become a less explicit (although not necessarily less important) element of the final stages of the mortuary rites. At the same time, there is an increased emphasis on a wider élite identity through the use of a new suite of dress items, an identity that appears to place a Christian identity, as reflected in the increased use of cross-imagery, to the fore.

It is important to remember that this rise in the use of Christian symbolism is not being promoted by the Church; as noted earlier, the Church appears to have taken a relatively laissez-faire approach to burial, and indeed to most of the key rites of passage at this period. Instead, these new responses to religion appear to be generated by and for women. Women appear to have taken a key role in the management and control of burial rites in Middle Anglo-Saxon England (Geake 2002), so we may expect that both the increased emphasis on Christianity within the graves and also the decreasing focus on objects which may have conveyed an alternate or completing identity were the responsibility of women themselves. Significantly, we do not see, at this stage, the exclusion of symbolic and amuletic objects, rather their redeployment in less obvious locations, and potentially increased control over public knowledge about the precise composition of these assemblages. The practice of concealment of certain classes of item suggests that those responsible for organisation of the mortuary rites are responsible for creating competing or alternative messages, which would have been apparent to different individuals in the funerary process. We have parallel discourses in play within the grave, an overt and public expression of Christianised elite status which runs alongside an alternative, even discrepant discourse about the continued significance of female gender roles, and even ritual power, in the construction of the grave assemblage. The grave is clearly a potent site for the redrawing and renegotiation of symbolic identities, or at least those connected to high-status females. Crucially, the foregrounding of Christian identity is not being driven by the church, but by female peer groups, potentially cross-cutting traditional secular/ecclesiastical divides.

The grave remains a field of discourse within which identities can be expressed, but through the on-going cultural practice of overseeing burial rites, these identities are seen to be plastic and capable of re-ordering and prioritisation, but not as prescribed by external ecclesiastical demands. Not surprisingly, there are regional variations in which these are made manifest; for example, 'thread boxes', small copper alloy cylinders, sometimes decorated with cross symbols, are found in many female graves in the mid- to late seventh century. It has convincingly been suggested that they functioned as containers for small personal relics, such as *brandea* (cloth that had been in contact with a primary relic). Although around 50 are known, their distribution is focused on east Kent, the Midlands and Northumbria. There is a notable absence from most of Wessex; it is possible that this may reflect different attitudes to sainthood in this region. Barbara Yorke has noted the lack of local saints in Wessex, and the absence of a tradition of a male saint in its royal house before Edward the Martyr (d. 978) (Yorke 2003, 251). It is possible that there is a connection between the lack of indigenous saints and the lack of 'thread-boxes', with the manifestation of sainthood and the cult of relics taking a different form here than in other kingdoms.

Whatever the underlying reason for this particular distribution pattern, the motive factor behind the changes in burial practice was seated within the burial community itself. New communities of converts are working with existing symbolic resources to fashion new religious identities, rather than passively receiving new cultural packages transmitted by the incoming ecclesiastical establishment. This potentially contrasts with male élite burials, which are far less visible; while they may simply be utilising a different range of options for expressing identity, a strong argument could be made that they are buryied within ecclesiastical establishments, one of the relatively few locations within Anglo-Saxon England, where the church was probably able to exercise direct control over burial rites. It may even be possible to see the move by men towards church burial as a deliberate attempt to cut themselves loose from female control of a key ritual activity, replacing the dominant role of female ritual specialists with an alternate mode of control predicated on close relationships with the burgeoning Church.

We see highly gendered responses to the way in which Christianity was being mediated through the funerary domain; women acting creatively to construct a mortuary identity, which while expressing some element of Christianity, was more focused on perpetuating a common, although gendered, elite identity. Within this burial rite, the concealed placement of other symbolic and amuletic objects undercut or at least acted as a counterpoint to the more explicit identities being demonstrated. Men, meanwhile, were seeking more direct relationships with the church in death, and potentially subordinating their own agency in the burial act to Christian religious specialists.

Conclusion

This brief consideration of the way in which Christianity might have been represented and expressed in seventh-century Anglo-Saxon England has been only a partial attempt to outline how an archaeology of the conversion process might appear. It has not addressed many key topics; I have made no mention of church architecture or stone sculpture, for example, two areas of major cultural innovation in the first hundred years following the arrival of the Augustinian mission. Obviously any attempt to develop a truly comprehensive archaeological narrative would need to be many times longer than this book. However, what I hope I have done is to begin to show how some of the conceptual challenges I have raised in this book might be addressed in practice. I have tried to move beyond the notion of 'intellectual communities' or 'micro-Christendoms' to suggest that many of the variations within the ways in which Christianity was adopted reflect faultlines within, as well as between, societies. By considering the differences between the funerary rites of high-status males and females I have attempted to bring into focus other axes of analysis, such as gender, that might reflect varying modes of reception of Christianity. Importantly, I also argue that changes in burial rite are not simply passive reactions to the arrival of the new faith, but carefully constructed responses to these religious changes, building new identities out of the new symbolic repertoires provided by the Church, but also incorporating existing pre-Christian modes of expressing identity.

There was no decision to avoid referring to the documentary evidence for this period in my analysis. However, this demonstrates, not that historical sources are irrelevant (they most certainly are not), but that it is possible to explore Christianity and conversion from a primarily archaeological perspective, recentring the role of material culture and materiality in the study of this crucial period of religious change. There are also, doubtless, some conceptual challenges thrown down in the preceding chapters that require a more detailed engagement with our existing set of archaeological methodologies if they are to translate into practical ways forward. However, the title of this series of volumes is 'Debates in Archaeology', and I can only hope that I have been able to set out the lines of the debates that need to be addressed by scholars exploring the process of early medieval religious change, providing them with new ways of looking and thinking about the material on which they work.

Bibliography

Alcock, L. 1963. *Dinas Powys: An Iron Age, Dark Age and Early Medieval Settlement in Glamorgan*. Cardiff: University of Wales Press.

Aldhouse Green, M. 1999. *Pilgrims in Stone: Stone Images from the Gallo-Roman Sanctuary of Fontes Sequanae*. Oxford: BAR (Int. Ser.) 754.

Andrén, A. 1998. *Between Artefacts and Texts. Historical Archaeology in Global Perspective*. New York: Plenum Press.

Andrén, A., Jennbert, K. and Raudvere, C. (eds) 2006. *Old Norse Religion in Long-Term Perspectives*. Lund: Nordic Academic Press.

Arnold, C. 1983. 'The Sancton-Baston potter [die-stamps and fabric]', *Scottish Archaeological Review* 2: 17-30.

Arnold, C.J. 1988. *An Archaeology of the Early Anglo-Saxon Kingdoms*. London: Routledge.

Artelius, T. and Svanberg, F. 2007. *Dealing with the Dead: Archaeological Perspectives on Prehistoric Scandinavian Burial Ritual*. Riksantikvarieämbetets Forlag.

Asad, T. 1973. *Anthropology and the Colonial Encounter*. London: Ithaca Press.

Barford, P. 2002. 'East is East and West is West? Power and paradigm in European archaeology', in P. Biehl, A. Gramsch and A. Marciniak (eds) *Archäologien Europas/ Archaeologies of Europe*. Tubingen: Waxman, 77-98.

Barker, J. 1993. ' "We are Eklesia": conversion in Uiaku, Papua New Guinea', in R. Hefner (ed.) 1993b, 199-230.

Barrett, J.C. 1990. 'The monumentality of death: the character of Early Bronze Age mortuary mounds in southern Britain', *World Archaeology* 22(2), 179-89.

Barrett, J.C. 1991. 'Towards an archaeology of ritual', in P. Garwood, D. Jennings, R. Skeates and J. Toms (eds) *Sacred and Profane: Proceedings of a Conference on Archaeology, Ritual and Religion* Oxford, 1-10

Barrett, J.C. 1994. *Fragments from Antiquity: An Archaeology of Social Life 2900-1200 BC*. Oxford: Blackwell.

Barrett, J.C. 2000a. 'A thesis on agency', in M.-A. Dobres and J.E. Robb (eds) *Agency in Archaeology*. London: Routledge, 61-8.

Barrett, J.C. 2000b. 'Fields of discourse: reconstituting a social archaeology', in J. Thomas (ed.) *Interpretative Archaeology: A Reader*. London: Leicester University Press, 23-32.

Barrett, J.C. 2001. 'Agency, the duality of structure, and the problem of the archaeological record', in I. Hodder (ed.) *Archaeological Theory Today*. Cambridge: Polity, 141-64.

Barrowclough, D. and Malone, C. 2007. *Cult in Context: Reconsidering Ritual in Archaeology*. Oxford: Oxbow.

Bartlett, R. 1993. *The Making of Europe: Conquest, Colonization and Cultural Change, 950-1350*. Harmondsworth: Penguin.

Bartlett, R. 2007. 'From paganism to Christianity in medieval Europe', in N. Berend (ed.) 2007, 46-72.

Bedingfield, B. 2002. *The Dramatic Liturgy of Anglo-Saxon England*. Woodbridge: Boydell and Brewer.

Bell, C. 1995. *Ritual Theory; Ritual Practice*. Oxford: OUP.

Bell, C. 1997. *Ritual: Perspectives and Dimensions*. Oxford: OUP.

Bender, B., Hamilton, S. and Tilley, C. 1997. 'Leskernick: stone worlds; alternative narratives; nested landscapes', *Proceedings of the Prehistoric Society* 63, 147-78.

Berend, N. 2001. *At the Gate of Christendom: Jews, Muslims and 'pagans' in medieval Hungary, c.1000-c.1301*. Cambridge: CUP.

Berend, N. (ed.) 2007. *Christianisation and the Rise of Christian Monarchy*. Cambridge: CUP.

Berend, N., Laszlovszky, J. and Szakács, B. 2007. 'The Kingdom of Hungary', in N. Berend (ed.) 2007, 319-68.

Bergman, I. 2006. 'Indigenous time, colonial history: Sami conceptions of time and ancestry and the role of relics in cultural reproduction', *Norwegian Archaeological Review* 39/2, 151-61.

Bergren, A. and Nilsson Stutz, L. 2010. 'From spectator to critic and participant: a new role for archaeology in ritual studies', *Journal of Social Archaeology* 10, 171-97.

Birbeck, V. 2005. *The Origins of Mid-Saxon Southampton: Excavations at the Friends Provident St Mary's Stadium 1998-2000*. Salisbury: Trust for Wessex Archaeology.

Blair, J. 2005. *The Church in Anglo-Saxon Society*. Oxford: Blackwell.

Bloch, M. 1977. 'The past and the present in the present', *Man* (N.S.) 12, 278-92.

Bibliography

Bloch, M. 1985. 'From cognition to ideology', in R. Fardon (ed.) *Power and Knowledge: Anthropological and Sociological Approaches*. Edinburgh: Scottish Academic Press, 21-48.

Blomkvist, N. 2005. *The Discovery of the Baltic: The Reception of a Catholic World-system in the European North (AD 1075-1225)*. Leiden: Brill.

Bowie, F. 2000. *The Anthropology of Religion*. London: Routledge.

Bowles, C.R. 2007. *Rebuilding the Britons: The Postcolonial Archaeology of Culture and Identity in the Late Antique Bristol Channel Region*. Oxford: BAR 452.

Bourdieu, P. 1991. *A Logic of Practice*. Cambridge: CUP.

Boyle, A., Jennings, D and Scott, I. (eds) 1995. *Two Oxfordshire Anglo-Saxon Cemeteries: Berinsfield and Didcot*. Oxford: Oxford Archaeological Unit.

Boyle, A. et al. 1998. *The Anglo-Saxon Cemetery at Butler's Field, Lechlade, Gloucestershire I*, Oxford: Oxford Archaeological Unit.

Boyle, A., Hacking, P., Allen, T. and Ambers, J. 2002. 'The Anglo-Saxon grave from Boveney', in S. Foreman, J. Hiller and D. Petts (eds) 2002. *Gathering the People, Settling the Land: The Archaeology of a Middle Thames Landscape: Anglo-Saxon to Post-medieval*. Thames Valley Landscape Monograph 14. Oxford: Oxford Archaeology, 28-34.

Bradley, R. 1987. 'Time regained: the creation of continuity', *Journal of the British Archaeology Association* 140: 1-17.

Bradley, R. 1998a. *The Significance of Monuments*, London: Routledge.

Bradley, R. 1998b. *The Passage of Arms: An Archaeological Analysis of Prehistoric Hoards and Votive Deposits*, 2nd edn. Oxford: Oxbow.

Bradley, R. 2006. 'Can archaeologists study prehistoric cosmology?', in A. Andrén, K. Jennbert and C. Rautvere (eds) *Old Norse Religion in Long-term Perspective*. Lund: Nordic Academic Press, 16-20.

Bradley, R. and Edmonds, M. 1993. *Interpreting the Axe Trade: Production and Exchange in Neolithic Britain*. Cambridge: CUP.

Brantley, J. 2007. *Reading in the Wilderness: Private Devotion and Public Performance in Late Medieval England*. Chicago: University of Chicago Press.

Brogiolo, G. and Ward-Perkins, B. (eds) 1999. *The Idea and Ideal of the Town Between Late Antiquity and the Early Middle Ages*. Leiden: Brill.

Brown, P. 1970. 'Sorcery, demons and the rise of Christianity: from late Antiquity into the Middle Ages', in *Witchcraft Confessions and Accusations*. Association of Social Anthropologists Monographs 9, 17-45.

Bibliography

Brown, P. 1971. 'The rise and function of the holy man in late antiquity', *Journal of Roman Studies* 61, 80-101.

Brown, P. 1981. *The Cult of the Saints: Its Rise and Function in Latin Christianity*. Chicago: Chicago University Press.

Brown, P. 1988. *The Body and Society: Men, Women, and Sexual Renunciation in Early Christianity*. New York: Columbia University Press.

Brown, P. 1992. *Power and Persuasion in Late Antiquity*. Madison, WI: University of Wisconsin Press.

Brown, P. 1996. *The Rise of Western Christendom* Oxford: Blackwell.

Brück, J. 1999. 'Ritual and rationality: some problems of interpretation in European archaeology', *European Journal of Archaeology* 2, 313-44.

Brunaux, J.-L. 1988. *The Celtic Gauls: Gods, Rites and Sanctuaries*. London: Seaby.

Buc, P. 2001. *The Dangers of Ritual: Between Early Medieval Texts and Social Scientific Theory*. Princeton: Princeton University Press.

Buko, A. 2008. *The Archaeology of Early Medieval Poland*. Leiden: Brill.

Bullough, D. 1983. 'Burial, community and belief in the early medieval west', in P. Wormald (ed.) *Ideal and Reality in Frankish and Anglo-Saxon Society*. Oxford: OUP, 177-201.

Burgess, B. 1886. 'Opening of a tumulus at Taplow', *Records of Buckinghamshire* 5, 331-5.

Burke, P. 1969. *The Renaissance Sense of the Past*. London: Edward Arnold.

Cameron, A. 1979. 'Images and authority; elites and icons in late sixth-century Byzantium', *Past and Present* 84, 3-35.

Cameron, A. 1993. *The Mediterranean World in Late Antiquity*. London: Routledge.

Camille, M. 1985. 'Seeing and reading: some visual implications of medieval literacy and illiteracy', *Art History* 8, 26-49.

Carver, M. 1993. *Arguments in Stone: Archaeological Research and the European Town in the First Millennium*. Oxford: Oxbow Books.

Carver, M. 1998a 'Conversion and politics on the eastern seaboard of Britain: some archaeological indicators', in B. Crawford (ed.) *Conversion and Christianity in the North Sea World*. University of St Andrew's, 11-40.

Carver, M. 1998b. *Sutton Hoo: Burial Ground of Kings*. London: British Museum Press.

Bibliography

Carver, M. 2001. 'Why that, why there, why then? The politics of early medieval monumentality', in A. Macgregor and H. Hamerow (eds) *Image and Power in Early Medieval British Archaeology: Essays in Honour of Rosemary Cramp*. Oxford: Oxbow Books, 1-22.

Carver, M. 2002. 'Reflections on the meaning of Anglo-Saxon barrows', in S. Lucy and A. Reynolds (eds) *Burial in Early Medieval England and Wales*. London: Society for Medieval Archaeology, 132-43.

Carver, M. 2003. *The Cross Goes North: Processes of Conversion in Northern Europe AD 300-1300*. Woodbridge: Boydell.

Carver, M. 2005. *Sutton Hoo: A Seventh-century Princely Burial Ground and its Context*. London: British Museum.

Carver, M. 2009. 'Early Scottish monasteries and prehistory: a preliminary dialogue', *Scottish Historical Review* 88/2, 332-51.

Carver, M. forthcoming. 'Intellectual communities in early Northumbria', in D. Petts and S. Turner (eds) *Early Medieval Northumbria: Kingdom and Communities*. Turnhout: Brepols.

Chadwick. N. 1966. *The Druids*. Cardiff, University of Wales Press.

Childe, V.G. 1956. *Piecing Together the Past*. London: Routledge.

Christiansen, E. 1997. *The Northern Crusades*, 2nd edn. Harmondsworth: Penguin.

Chronicle of Henry of Livonia = J.A. Brundage (ed. & tr.) 1961. *The Chronicle of Henry of Livonia*. Madison, WI: University of Wisconsin Press.

Chronicon = D.A. Warner (ed. & tr.) 2001. *Ottonian Germany: The Chronicle of Thietmar of Merseburg*. Manchester: Manchester University Press.

Chuvin, P. 1990: *A Chronicle of the Last Pagans*, Cambridge, MA: Harvard University Press.

Clay, J.-H. 2009. 'Sacred landscapes and the conversion of eighth-century Hessia', *Landscapes* 9.2, 1-25.

Clunies Ross, Margaret. 2006a. 'The cultural politics of the Skaldic ekphrasis poem in medieval Norway and Iceland', in H. Fulton, R. Evans and D. Matthews (eds) *Medieval Cultural Studies*. Cardiff: University of Wales Press, 227-40.

Cohn, B.S. 1996. *Colonialism and its Forms of Knowledge*. Princeton: Princeton University Press.

Coleman, S. and Elsner, J. 1994. 'The pilgrim's progress: art, architecture and ritual movement at Sinai', *World Archaeology* 26, 73-84.

Coleman, S. and Elsner, J. 1995. *Pilgrimage: Past and Present in the World Religions*. London: British Museum Press.

Comaroff, J. and Comaroff, J. 1986. 'Christianity and colonialism in South Africa', *American Ethnologist* 13, 1-22.

Comaroff, J. and Comaroff, J. 1991. *Of Revelation and Revolution: Christianity, Colonialism and Consciousness in South Africa*. Chicago: Chicago University Press..

Confessio = A.B.E. Hood (ed. & tr.) 1978. *St Patrick: His Writings and Muirchu's Life*. Chichester: Philimore.

Conolly, S. and Picard, J.-M. 'Cogitosus: Life of St Brigid', *Journal of the Royal Society of Antiquaries of Ireland* 117, 5-27.

Content, S. and Williams, H. 2010. 'Creating the pagan English', in M. Carver et al. (eds) 2010. *Signals of Belief in Early England: Anglo-Saxon Paganism Revisited*. Oxford: Oxbow Books, 181-200.

Cookson, N. 1987. 'The Christian Church in Roman Britain: a synthesis of archaeology', *World Archaeology* 18, 426-33.

Cox Miller, P. 2009. 'On the edge of self and other: holy bodies in late antiquity', *Journal of Early Christian Studies* 17/2, 171-93.

Crawford, S. 2004. 'Votive deposition, religion and the Anglo-Saxon furnished burial rite', *World Archaeology* 36(1), 83-102.

Cunliffe, B. and Davenport, P. 1985. *The Temple of Sulis Minerva at Bath*. Oxford University Committee for Archaeology Monograph 7.

Curta, F. 2001. 'Pots, Slavs, and "imagined communities": Slavic archaeology and the history of the early Slavs', *European Journal of Archaeology* 4/3, 367-84.

Curta, F. 2005. 'Introduction', in F. Curta (ed.) *Borders, Barriers, and Ethnogenesis: Frontiers in Late Antiquity and the Middle Ages*, Studies in the Early Middle Ages 12. Turnhout: Brepols, 1-9.

Curta, F. 2007. 'Some remarks on ethnicity in medieval archaeology', *Early Medieval Europe* 15(2), 159-85.

Curta, F. 2009. 'The history and archaeology of Great Moravia: an introduction', *Early Medieval Europe* 17(3), 238-47.

Cusack, C. 1998. *The Rise of Christianity in Northern Europe 300-1000*. London: Cassell.

de Bhaldraithe, E. 1991. 'Appendix: strainers and other instruments in early church ritual', in Watts 1991, 231-33.

Davies, W. 1982.'The Latin charter tradition in Western Britain, Brittany and Ireland in the early medieval period', in D. Dumville, R. McKitterick and D. Whitelock (eds) *Ireland in Early Medieval Europe*. Cambridge: CUP, 258-81.

Davies, W. 1992. 'The myth of the Celtic church', in N. Edwards and A. Lane (eds) *The Early Church in Wales and the West* Oxford: Oxbow Books, 12-22.

Bibliography

De Civitate Dei = H. Bettenson (ed. & tr.) 1972. *Augustine: Concerning the City of God*. Harmondsworth: Penguin.

*De Cura Gerenda Pro Mortui*s = J. Lacey (ed. & tr.) 1955. 'The care to be taken for the dead', in *St Augustine: Treatises on Marriage and Other Subjects*. The Fathers of the Church 27.

Devlin, Z. 2007. *Remembering the Dead in Anglo-Saxon England: Memory Theory in Archaeology and History*. Oxford: BAR 446.

Dobson, L. 2008. Landscape, Monuments and the Construction of Social Power in Early Medieval Deira. Unpublished PhD dissertation, University of York.

Driscoll, S.T. 1988. 'The relationship between history and archaeology: artefacts, documents and power', in S.T. Driscoll and M.R. Nieke (eds) *Power and Politics in Early Medieval Britain and Ireland*. Edinburgh: Edinburgh University Press, 162-87.

Driscoll, S. 1998. 'Picts and prehistory: cultural resource management in early medieval Scotland', *World Archaeology* 30, 142-58.

Duggan, L.G. 1989. 'Was art really the book of the illiterate?', *Word and Image* 5, 227-51.

Durkheim, E. 1976. *The Elementary Forms of the Religious Life*. London: George Allen (originally published 1915).

Edwards, N. 1998. 'Two carved stone pillars from Trefollwyn, Anglesey', *Archaeological Journal* 154, 108-17.

Edwards, N. 2001. 'Early medieval inscribed stones and stone sculpture in Wales: context and function', *Medieval Archaeology* 45, 15-39.

Edwards, N. 2007. *A Corpus of Early Medieval Inscribed Stones and Stone Sculpture in Wales,* vol. II: *South-West Wales*, Cardiff: University of Wales Press.

Effros, B. 1997, 'De partibus Saxoniae and the regulation of mortuary custom: a Carolingian campaign of Christianization or the suppression of Saxon identity?', *Revue Belge de Philologie et d'Histoire* 75, 267-86.

Eihmane, E. 2009. 'The Baltic crusades: a clash of two identities', in A. Murray (ed.) 2009, 37-52.

Elsner, J. 1995. *Art and the Roman Viewer: The Transformation of Art from the Pagan World to Christianity*, Cambridge, New York and Melbourne: CUP.

Esmonde Cleary, S. 2001. 'The Roman to medieval transition', in M. Millett and S. James (eds) *Britons and Romans: Advancing an Archaeological Agenda*. CBA Research Report 125, 90-7.

Evans, A.C. 1986. *The Sutton Hoo Ship Burial*. London: British Museum Press.

Bibliography

Evans, J., Chenery, C. and Fitzpatrick, A.P. 2006. 'Bronze age childhood migration of individuals near Stonehenge, revealed by strontium and oxygen isotope tooth enamel analysis', *Archaeometry*, 48 (2), 309-21.

Faulkner, N. 2003. 'The debate about the end: a review of evidence and methods', *Antiquaries Journal* 159, 59-76.

Faur, J. 1978. 'The biblical idea of idolatry', *Jewish Quarterly Review* vol. 69, no. 1 (July 1978), 1-15.

Filmer-Sankey, W. and Pestell, T. 2000. *Snape Anglo-Saxon Cemetery: Excavations and Surveys 1824-1992.* East Anglian Archaeology Report 95.

Flanigan, C., Ashley, K. and Sheingorn, P. 2005. 'Liturgy as social performance: expanding the definitions', in T. Heffernan and E. Matter (eds) *The Liturgy of the Medieval Church.* Kalamazoo: Medieval Institute Publications, 635-52.

Fletcher, R. 1997. *The Conversion of Europe: From Paganism to Christianity 371-1386 AD.* London, HarperCollins.

Fogelin, L. (ed.) 2008. *Religion, Archaeology and the Material World.* Carbondale Occasional Papers, Carbondale: Southern Illinois University Press.

Forsyth, K. 1998. 'Literacy in Pictland', in H. Pryce (ed.) *Literacy in Medieval Celtic Societies.* Cambridge: CUP, 39-62.

Forsyth, K. 2007. 'An ogham-inscribed plaque from Bornais, South Uist', in B. Ballin-Smith, S. Taylor and G. Williams (eds) *West over Sea: Studies in Scandinavian Sea-borne Expansion and Settlement before 1300. A Festschrift in honour of Dr Barbara E. Crawford.* Leiden: Brill, 460-77.

Frend, W.H.C. 1984-5. 'Syrian parallels to the Water Newton treasure', *Jahrbuch für Antike und Christentum* 27-8, 146-50.

Frend, W.H.C. 1996. *Archaeology of Early Christianity.* London: Geoffrey Chapman.

Frend, W.H.C. 1999. 'Archaeology and library work in the study of early Christianity', in T. Insoll (ed.) 1999, 182-7.

Fulford, M. and Rippon, S. 1994. 'Lowbury Hill, Oxon: a re-assessment of the portable Romano-Celtic temple and the Anglo-Saxon barrow', *Archaeological Journal* 151, 158-211.

Gallic Wars = C. Hammond (tr.) *Julius Caesar: Seven Commentaries on the Gallic War.* Oxford: OUP.

Gane, R.E. 2004. *Ritual Dynamic Structure.* Gorgias Dissertations 14, Religion 1.

Gáspár, D. 2002. *Christianity in Roman Pannonia: An Evaluation of*

Bibliography

Early Christian Finds and Sites from Hungary with a Fully Illustrated Catalogue. Oxford: BAR (i)1010.

Gauthier, N. 1999. 'La topographie chretienne entre ideologie et pragmatisme', in Brogiolo and Ward-Perkins (eds) 1999, 195-209.

Geake, H. 1997. *The Use of Grave-Goods in Conversion-period England*. Oxford: BAR 261.

Geake, H. 1999. 'Invisible kingdoms: the use of grave-goods in seventh-century England', in T.M. Dickinson and D. Griffiths (eds) *The Making of Kingdoms*. Anglo-Saxon Studies in Archaeology and History 10.

Geake, H. 2002. 'Persistent problems in the study of conversion period burials in England', in A. Reynolds and S. Lucy (eds) 2002, 144-55.

Geary, P.J. 'Ethnic identity as a situational construct in the Early Middle Ages', *Mitteilungen der anthropologischen Gesellschaft in Wien* 113, 15-26.

Gell, A. 1992. *The Anthropology of Time: Cultural Constructions of Temporal Maps and Images*. Oxford: Berg.

Gerrard, C.M. 2003. *Medieval Archaeology: Understanding Traditions and Contemporary Approaches*. London, Routledge.

Giddens, A. 1979. *Central Problems in Social Theory*. London: Macmillan.

Gilchrist, R. 1988. 'The spatial archaeology of gendered domains: a case study of English nunneries', *Archaeological Review of Cambridge* 7, 21-8.

Gilchrist, R. 1994. *Gender and Material Culture: The Archaeology of Religious Women*. London: Routledge.

Gilchrist, R. 2008. 'Magic for the dead? The archaeology of magic in later medieval burials', *Medieval Archaeology* 52, 119-60.

Gilchrist, R. 2009. 'Medieval archaeology and theory: a disciplinary leap of faith', in R. Gilchrist and A. Reynolds (eds) *Reflections: 50 Years of Medieval Archaeology 1957-2007*. Society for Medieval Archaeology Monograph 30, Leeds, 385-408.

Gill, M. 2001. 'The role of images in monastic education: the evidence from wall paintings in late medieval England', in G. Ferzoco and C. Muessig (eds) *Medieval Monastic Education*. Leicester University Press, 117-35.

Glick, T. 2001. *Islamic and Christian Spain in the Early Middle Ages*. Leiden: Brill.

Goody, J. 1977. *Domestication of the Savage Mind*. Cambridge: CUP.

Gosden, C. 1994. *Social Being and Time: An Archaeological Perspective*. Blackwell, Oxford.

Bibliography

Gosden, C. and Lock, G. 1998. 'Prehistoric histories', *World Archaeology* 30, 2-12.

Grabar, O. 1967. *The Beginnings of Christian Art, 200-395 AD*. London: Thames & Hudson.

Gräsland, A.-S. 1981. *Birka IV: The Burial Customs*. Stockholm: The Birka Project.

Graves, P. 1989. 'Social space in the English parish church', *Economy and Society* 18 (3), 297-322.

Graves, P. 2007. 'Sensing and believing: exploring worlds of difference in pre-modern England – a contribution to the debate', *World Archaeology* 39(4): 515-31.

Green, M. 1992. *The World of the Druids*. London: Thames & Hudson.

Habbe, P. 2006. 'How to sort out ritual from context of practice', in A. Andrén et al. (eds), 92-4.

Hadley, D. 2000. 'Equality, humility and non-materialism? Christianity and Anglo-Saxon burial practices', *Archaeological Review from Cambridge* 17:2, 149-78.

Halsall, G. 1995. *Early Medieval Cemeteries: An Introduction to Burial Archaeology in the Post-Roman West*. Glasgow: Cruithne Press.

Halsall, G. 2001. 'Childeric's grave, Clovis' succession, and the origins of the Merovingian Kingdom', in R.W. Mathiesen and D. Shanzer (eds) *Society and Culture in Late Antique Gaul: Revisiting the Sources*. Aldershot: Ashgate, 116-33.

Halsall, G. 2007. *Barbarian Migrations and the Roman West, 376-568*. Cambridge: CUP.

Hamerow, H. 2006. 'Special deposits in Anglo-Saxon settlements', *Medieval Archaeology* 50, 1-30.

Handley, M. 2001. 'The origins of Christian commemoration in late antique Britain', *Early Medieval Europe* 10, 177-99.

Harries, J. 1992: 'Christianity and the city in Gaul', in J. Rich (ed.) *The City in Late Antiquity*, London: Routledge, 77-98.

Harrison, K. 1976. *The Framework of Anglo-Saxon History to A.D. 900*. Cambridge: CUP.

Hawkes, C. 1954. 'Archaeological theory and method: some suggestions from the Old World', *American Anthropologist* 56, 155-68.

HE = L. Sherley-Price (tr.) 1988. Bede, *A History of the English Church and People*. Harmondsworth: Penguin.

Hefner, R. 1987. 'The political economy of Islamic conversion in modern East Java', in W.R. Roff (ed.) *Islam and the Political Economy of Meaning*. London: Routledge, 53-78.

Bibliography

Hefner, R.W. 1993a. 'The rationality of conversion' in R.W. Hefner (ed.) 3-46.

Hefner, R.W. (ed.) 1993b. *Conversion to Christianity: Historical and Anthropological Perspectives on a Great Transformation.* Berkeley, CA: University of California Press.

Henig, M. 1984. *Religion in Roman Britain.* London: Batsford.

Herbord, *Dialogus de vita sancti Ottonis episcopi Babenbergensis*, ed. J. Wirkarjak and K. Liman. 1973. MPH ns 7/3, Warsaw.

Herrin, J. 1987. *The Formation of Christendom.* Princeton: Princeton University Press.

Higham, N.J. 1997. *The Convert Kings.* Manchester: Manchester University Press.

Hill, J.D. 1995. *Ritual and Rubbish in the Iron Age of Wessex: A Study on the Formation of a Specific Archaeological Record.* Oxford: BAR 242.

Hiltebeitel, A. 1991. 'Of camphor and coconuts', *Wilson Quarterly* 28.

Hodder, I. 1982. *The Present Past: An Introduction to Anthropology for Archaeologists.* London: Batsford.

Hodder, I. 1990. *The Domestication of Europe: Structure and Contingency in Neolithic Societies.* Oxford: Blackwell.

Hodder, I. and Hutson, S. 2005. *Reading the Past: Current Approaches to Interpretation in Archaeology*, 3rd edn. Cambridge: Cambridge University Press.

Hodges, R. 1982. *Dark Age Economics.* London: Duckworth.

Høilund Nielsen, K. 1999. 'Style II and the Anglo-Saxon élite', in T.M. Dickinson and D. Griffiths (eds) *Anglo-Saxon Studies in Archaeology and History* 10, Oxford: Oxford University School of Archaeology.

Hopkins, K.1998. 'Early Christian numbers and its implications', *Journal of Early Christian Studies* 6/2, 185-226.

Hopkins, K. 1999. *A World Full of Gods: Pagans, Jews and Christians in the Roman World.* London: Phoenix.

Horton, R. 1975. 'African conversion', *Africa* 41, 85-108.

Horton, R. 1975. 'On the rationality of conversion', *Africa* 45, 219-55 (part 1) and 373-99 (part 2).

Howlett, D. 1995. *The Celtic Latin Tradition of Biblical Style.* Dublin: Four Courts Press.

Hultgard, A. 1991. 'Old Scandinavian and Christian eschatology', in T. Ahlbäck (ed.) *Old Norse and Finnish Religions and Cultic Place-Names.* Stockholm: Almqvist & Wiksell, 344-57.

Bibliography

Hultkranz, A. 1980. 'Christian influence on Northern Algonkian eschatology', *Sciences Religieuses / Studies in Religion* 9, 161-83.

Hyslop, M. 1963. 'Two Anglo-Saxon cemeteries at Chamberlains Barn, Leighton Buzzard', *Bedfordshire Archaeological Journal* 120, 161-200.

Ikenga-Metuh, E. 1987. 'The shattered microcosm: a critical survey of explanations of conversion in Africa', in K. Holst Petersen (ed.) *Religion, Development and African Identity*. Uppsala: Scandinavian Institute of African Studies, 11-27.

Insoll, T. 1999. *The Archaeology of Islam*. Oxford: Blackwell.

Insoll, T. 2004. *Archaeology, Ritual and Religion*. London: Routledge.

Jenkins, D. (ed. & tr.) 2000. *The Law of Hywel Dda: Law Texts from Medieval Wales*. Llandysul, Gomer Press.

Jennbert, K. 2000. 'Archaeology and pre-Christian religion in Scandinavia', *Current Swedish Archaeology* 8, 127-43.

de Jong, M. 2006. 'Ecclesia and the early medieval polity', in S. Airlie, W. Pohl and H. Reimitz (eds) *Staat im frühen Mittelalter*. Wien: Verlag der Österreichischen Akademie der Wissenschaften.

Jones, S. 1997. *The Archaeology of Ethnicity: A Theoretical Perspective*. London: Routledge.

Jonuks, T. 2005. 'Archaeology of religion: possibilities and prospects', *Estonian Journal of Archaeology* 9(1), 32-59.

Jonuks, T. 2009. '*Hiis* sites in the research history of Estonian sacred sites', *Folklore* 42 http://www.folklore.ee/folklore/vol42/jonuks.pdf [accessed 2/5/2010].

Jorgensen, L. 2003. 'Manor and market at Lake Tisso in the sixth to eleventh centuries: the Danish "productive" site', in T. Pestell and K. Ulmschneider (eds) *Markets in Early Medieval Europe. Trading and 'Productive' Sites, 650-850*. Bollington: Windgather Press, 177-207.

Kaliff, A. 2007. *Fire, Water, Heaven and Earth: Ritual Practice and Cosmology in Ancient Scandinavia – An Indo-European Perspective*. Riksantikvarieämbetets Forlag.

Kendall, C., Nicholson, O., Phillips, W. and Ragnow, M. (eds) 2009. *Conversion to Christianity from late Antiquity to the Modern Age*. Minnesota Studies in Early Modern History 1.

Kilbride, W. 2000. 'Why I feel cheated by the term Christianisation', in A.G. Pluskowski (ed.) *Early Medieval Religion: Archaeological Review from Cambridge* 17:2, 1-17.

Kitzinger, E. 1954. 'The cult of the images in the period before iconoclasm', *Dumbarton Oak Papers* 8, 85-150.

Kloczowski, J. 1993. 'La nouvelle chrétienté du monde occidental: la

Bibliography

christianisation des Slaves, des Scandinaves et des Hongrois entre le IXe et le XIe siècle', in G. Dagron (ed.) *Histoire du Christianisme des origins à nos jours*, vol. 4, Paris, 869-908.

Knight, J.K. 1999. *The End of Antiquity: Archaeology, Society and Religion AD 235-700*. Stroud: Tempus.

Krautheimer, R. 1986. *Early Christian and Byzantine Architecture*. Harmondsworth: Penguin.

Kristiansen, K. 1984. 'Ideology and material culture: an archaeological perspective', in M. Spriggs (ed.) *Marxist Perspectives in Archaeology*. Cambridge: CUP, 101-7.

Kujit, I. 2001. 'Place, death and the transmission of social memory in early agricultural communities of Near Eastern pre-pottery Neolithic', in M.S. Chesson (ed.) *Social Memory, Identity and Death: Anthropological Perspectives on Mortuary Rituals*. Arlington: American Anthropological Association, 80-99.

Kyriakidis, E. 2007. *The Archaeology of Ritual*. Los Angeles: Cotsen Institute of Archaeology.

Lapidus, I. 1988. *A History of Islamic Societies*. Cambridge: CUP.

Lapidge, M. 1984. 'Gildas's education and the Latin culture of sub-Roman Britain', in D. Dumville and M. Lapidge (eds) 1984. *Gildas: New Approaches*. Woodbridge: Boydell Press.

Life of Saint Martin = C. White (ed.) 1998. *Early Christian Lives*. Harmondsworth: Penguin, 134-59.

Larsson, L. and Lenntorp, K.-M. 2004. 'The enigmatic house', in L. Larsson (ed.) *Continuity for Centuries. A Ceremonial Building and its Context at Uppåkra, Southern Sweden*. Uppåkrastudier 10/Acta Archaeologica Lundensia, Series in 8?, 48. Stockholm: Almqvist & Wiksell, 3-48.

Leahy, K. 2007. *The Anglo-Saxon Kingdom of Lindsey*. Stroud: Tempus.

Letters = E. Emerton (ed. & tr.) 1940. *The Letters of Saint Boniface*. New York: Columbia University Press.

Livonian Rhymed Chronicle = J.C. Smith and W. Urban (ed. & tr.) 2001. *The Livonian Rhymed Chronicle*. Chicago: Lithuanian Research and Studies Center.

Longden, G. 2003. 'Iconoclasm, belief and memory in early medieval Wales', in H. Williams (ed.) *Archaeologies of Remembrance: Death and Memory in Past Societies*. New York: Kluwer/Plenum, 171-92.

Loosley, E. 1999. 'The early Syriac liturgical drama and its architectural setting', in Insoll (ed.) 1999, 18-25.

Loseby, S. and Christie, N. 1996. *Towns in Transition: Urban Evolu-*

tion in Late Antiquity and the Early Middle Ages. Aldershot: Ashgate.

Lucas, G. 2005. *The Archaeology of Time.* London: Routledge.

Lucy, S. 2000. *The Anglo-Saxon Way of Death: Burial Rites in Early England.* Stroud: Sutton.

Lucy, S. 2002. 'Burial practice in early medieval eastern England: constructing local indentities, deconstructing ethnicities', in S. Lucy and A. Reynolds (eds) 2002, 72-87.

Lucy, S. and Reynolds, A. (eds) 2002. *Burial in Early Medieval England and Wales.* Society for Medieval Archaeology Monograph Series 17, Leeds.

Lucy, S., Tipper, J and Dickens, A. 2009a. *The Anglo-Saxon Settlement and Cemetery at Bloodmoor Hill, Carlton Colville, Suffolk.* Cambridge Archaeological Unit, East Anglian Archaeology Report 131.

Lucy, S. et al. 2009b. 'The burial of a princess? The later seventh century at Westfield Farm, Ely', *Antiquaries Journal* 89, 81-141.

Lund, J. 2010. 'At the water's edge', in M. Carver et al. (eds) 2010, 49-66.

McCarthy, M.J. 2009. 'Modalities of belief in ancient Christian debate', *Journal of Early Christian Studies* 17:4, 605-34.

MacCormack, S. 1981. *Art and Ceremony in Late Antiquity,* Berkeley: University of California Press.

MacDonald, P. 2007. *Llyn Cerrig Bach: A Study of the Copper Alloy Artefacts from the Insular La Tene Assemblage.* Cardiff: University of Wales Press.

MacLeod, M. and Mees, B. 2006. *Runic Amulets and Magic Objects.* Woodbridge: Boydell.

McManus, D. 1997. *A Guide to Ogam.* Maynooth Monographs 4, An Sagart.

MacMullen, R. 1984. *Christianizing the Roman Empire (A.D. 100-400).* New Haven: Yale University Press.

MacMullen, R. 1985. 'Conversion: a historian's view', *The Second Century* 5:2, 67-81.

Mäesalu, A. and Valk, H. 2006. 'Research into the late Iron Age', in V. Lang (ed.) *Archaeological Research in Estonia 1865-2005.* Tartu: Tartu University Press.

Mainstone, R.J. 1988. *Hagia Sophia: Architecture, Structure and liturgy in Justinian's Great Church* London: Thames & Hudson.

Mägi, M. 2002. *At the Crossroads of Space and Time: Graves, Changing Society and ideology on Saaremaa (Ösel) 9th-13th centuries AD.* CCC Papers 6. Gotland.

Bibliography

Mägi, M. 2004. ' "Ships are their main strength": harbour sites, arable lands and chieftains on Saaremaa', *Estonian Journal of Archaeology* 8(2), 128-62.

Marciniak, A. 2006. 'Central European archaeology at the crossroads', in R. Layton, S. Shennan and P. Stone (eds). *A Future for Archaeology: The Past in the Present*, London: UCL Press, 157-72.

Markus, R. 1990. *The End of Ancient Christianity*. Cambridge: CUP.

Mayr-Harting, H. 1991. *The Coming of Christianity to Anglo-Saxon England*, 3rd edn. London: Batsford.

Meaney, A. 1964. *A Gazetteer of Early Anglo-Saxon Burial Sites*. London: Allen & Unwin,

Meaney, A. 1981. *Anglo-Saxon Amulets and Curing Stones*. Oxford: BAR 96.

Meaney, A. 1995. 'Pagan English sanctuaries, place-names and hundred meeting-places', *Anglo-Saxon Studies in Archaeology and History* 90, 29-48.

Meaney, A. and Hawkes, S.C. 1970. *Two Anglo-Saxon cemeteries at Winnall, Winchester, Hampshire London*, Society of Medieval Archaeology Monograph.

Mensching, G. 1964. 'Folk and universal religion', in L. Schneider (ed.) *Religion, Culture and Society: A Reader in the Sociology of Religion*. New York: Wiley, 254-61.

Migotti, B. 1997. *Evidence for Christianity in Roman Southern Pannonia (Northern Croatia): A Catalogue of Finds and Sites* Oxford: BAR (i) 684.

Mitchell, W.J. 1997. *Picture Theory: Essays in Verbal and Visual Representation*. Chicago: University of Chicago Press.

Mizoguchi, K. 1993. 'Time in the reproduction of mortuary practices', *World Archaeology* 25(2), 223-35.

MOLAS 2004. *The Prittlewell Prince: The Discovery of a Rich Anglo-Saxon Burial in Essex*. Museum of London Archaeological Service.

Moltke, K. 1985. *Runes and their Origins: Denmark and Elsewhere*, tr. P.G. Foote, Copenhagen.

Moreland, J. 2001. *Archaeology and Text*. London: Duckworth.

Moreland, J. 2006. 'Archaeology and text: subservience or enlightenment?' *Annual Review of Anthropology* 35, 135-51.

Morris, B. 1990. *Anthropological Studies of Religion*. Cambridge: CUP.

Munch, G., Johansen, O. and Roesdahl, E. 2003. *Borg in Lofoten: A Chieftain's Farm in North Norway*. Trondheim: Tapir Academic Press.

Bibliography

Munz, P. 1976, 'Early European history and African anthropology', *New Zealand Journal of History* 10, 33-48.

Murray, A. (ed.) 2009. *The Clash of Cultures on the Medieval Baltic Frontier*. Aldershot: Ashgate.

Mytum, H. 1989. 'Functionalist and non-functionalist approaches to monastic archaeology', in R. Gilchrist and H. Mytum (eds) *The Archaeology of Rural Monasteries*. Oxford: BAR 203, 339-61.

Mytum, H. 1992. *The Origins of Early Christian Ireland*. London: Routledge.

Mytum, H. 2006. 'Materiality and memory: an archaeological perspective on the popular adoption of linear time in Britain', *Antiquity* 81, 381-96.

Nielsen, A.-L. 1997. 'Pagan cult and votive acts at Borg. An expression of the central significance of the farmstead in the Late Iron Age', in H. Andersson, P. Carelli and L. Ersgård (eds) *Visions of the Past. Trends and Traditions in Swedish Medieval Archaeology*. Studies in Medieval Archaeology 19. Stockholm: Almqvist & Wiksell International, 373-92.

Nilsson-Stutz, L. 2008. 'Capturing mortuary ritual: an attempt to harmonise archaeological method and theory', in L. Fogelin (ed.) *Religion, Archaeology and the Material World*. Centre for Archaeological Investigations Occasional Paper no 36. Carbondale: Southern Illinois University Press, 159-78.

Nock, A.D. 1933. *Conversion: The Old and New in Religion from Alexander the Great to Augustine of Hippo*. Oxford: Clarendon Press.

Nordahl, E. 1996. *Templum quod Ubsola dicitur ... I arkeologisk belysning*. Uppsala: Deptartment of Archaeology.

Norr, S. 1998. *To Rede and To Rown: Expressions of Early Scandinavian Kingship in Written Sources*. Occasional Papers in Archaeology 17, Uppsala.

North, R. 2006. 'End time and the date of Voluspá: two models of conversion', in C. Karkov and Howe, N. (eds) *Conversion and Colonisation in Anglo-Saxon England*. Tempe, Arizona: Arizona Center for Medieval and Renaissance Studies, 213-36.

O Carragain, E. 2005. *Ritual and the Rood: Liturgical Images and the Old English Poems of the Dream of the Rood Tradition*. London: British Library.

O Carragain, T. 2009. 'The architectural setting of the Mass in early medieval Ireland', *Medieval Archaeology* 53, 119-54.

Olson, L. 1999. 'The applicability of the Horton African conversion to the conversion of medieval Europe', in C. Cusack and P. Old-meadow (eds). *This Immense Panorama: Studies in Honour of Eric J. Sharpe*. Sydney Studies in Religion 2 http://escholarship.usyd. edu.au/journals/index.php/SSR/article/viewFile/657/638 [accessed 1/5/10].

Orselli, A.M. 1999. 'L'idée chrétienne de la ville: quelques suggestions pour l'antiquité tardive et le haut moyen âge' in G. Brogiolo and B. Ward-Perkins (eds) 1999, 181-93.

O'Sullivan, D. 2001. 'Space silence and shortage on Lindisfarne: the archaeology of asceticism', in H. Hamerow and A. McGregor (eds) *Image and Power in the Archaeology of Early Medieval Britain: Essays in Honour of Rosemary Cramp*. Oxford: Oxbow Books, 33-52.

Painter, K.S. 1999. 'The Water Newton silver: votive or liturgical?', *Journal of British Archaeological Association* 152, 1-23.

Palmer, J. 2007. 'Defining paganism in the Carolingian world', *Early Medieval Europe* 15 (4), 402-25.

Parfitt, K. and Brugman, B. 1997. *The Anglo-Saxon Cemetery on Mill Hill, Deal, Kent*. London: Society for Medieval Archaeology Monograph 14.

Parker Pearson, M. 1982. 'Mortuary practices, society and ideology: an ethnoarchaeological study', in I. Hodder (ed.) *Symbolic and Structural Archaeology*. Cambridge: CUP, 99-113.

Paxton, F. 1990. *Christianizing Death: The Creation of a Ritual Process in Early Medieval Europe*. Ithaca, NY: Cornell University Press.

Pels, P. 1997. 'The anthropology of colonialism: culture, history and the emergence of Western governmentality', *Annual Review of Anthropology* 26, 163-83.

Penn, K. 2000. *Excavations on the Norwich Southern Bypass, 1989-91. Part II, The Anglo-Saxon Cemetery at Harford Farm, Caistor St Edmund, Norfolk*. East Anglian Archaeology Report 92.

Perring, D. 2003. ' "Gnosticism" in fourth century Britain: the Frampton mosaics reconsidered', *Britannia* 34, 97-127.

Petts, D. 2003. *Christianity in Roman Britain*. Stroud: Tempus.

Petts, D. 2003b 'Votive deposits and Christian practice in late Roman Britain', in M. Carver (ed.) 2003, 109-118.

Petts, D. 2009. *The Early Medieval Church in Wales*. Stroud: The History Press.

Pickles, C. 1999. *Texts and Monuments: A Study of Ten Anglo-Saxon Churches of the Pre-Viking Period*. Oxford: BAR 277.

Pluskowski, P. and Patrick, P. 2003. ' "How do you pray to God?"

Fragmentation and variety in early medieval Christianity', in M. Carver (ed.) 2003, 30-57.

Pohl, W. with Reimitz, P. (eds) 1998. *Strategies of Distinction: The Construction of Ethnic Communities, 300-800.* Leiden: Brill.

Poulton, R. and Scott, E. 1993. 'The hoarding, deposition and use of pewter in Roman Britain', *Theoretical Roman Archaeology: First Conference Proceedings.* Aldershot, 115-32.

Price, N. 2002. *The Viking Way: Religion and War in Late Iron Age Scandinavia.* Uppsala: Department of Archaeology and History.

Provost-Smith, P. 2009. 'The new Constantinianism: late antique paradigms and sixteenth-century strategies for the conversion of China', in C. Kendall et al. (eds) 2009, 223-58.

Pryce, H. 1993. *Native Law and the Church in Medieval Wales.* Oxford: OUP.

Rahtz, P.A. et al. 1992. *Cadbury-Congresbury 1968-73. A Late/Post-Roman Hilltop Settlement in Somerset.* Oxford: BAR 223.

Ranger, T. 1987. 'Taking hold of the land: holy places and pilgrimages in twentieth century Zimbabwe', *Past and Present* 117, 158-94.

Ranger, T. 1993. 'The local and the global in Southern African religious history', in R. Hefner (ed.) 1993b, 65-98.

Redknap, M. and Lewis, J. 2005. *A Corpus of Early Medieval Inscribed Stones and Stone Sculpture in Wales*, vol. 1: *Breconshire, Glamorgan, Monmouthshire, Radnorshire and Geographically Contiguous Areas of Herefordshire and Shropshire.* Cardiff: University of Wales Press.

Reventlow, H.G. 2001. 'The early church', in J. Rogerson (ed.) *The Oxford Illustrated History of the Bible.* Oxford: OUP, 166-80.

RGS 2010. 'Bronze Age Mediterraneans may have visited Stonehenge', http://www.bgs.ac.uk/research/highlights/bronzeAgeVisitors.html [accessed 12 September 2010].

Ross, A. 1968. 'Shafts, pits, wells – sanctuaries of the Belgic Britons', in J.M. Coles and D.D.A. Simpson (eds) *Studies in Ancient Europe: Essays Presented to Stuart Piggott.* Leicester University Press, 255-85.

Russell, J.C. 1994. *The Germanisation of Early Medieval Christianity: A Sociohistorical Approach to Religious Transformation.* Oxford: OUP.

Said, E. 1994. *Empire and Imperialism.* London: Verso.

Sanneh, L. 1989. *Translating the Message: The Missionary Impact on Culture.* Maryknoll, New York: Orbis Books.

Bibliography

Sayer, D. 2010. 'Death and the family: developing generational chronologies', *Journal of Social Archaeology* 10(1), 59-91.

Sanmark, A. 2004. *Power and Conversion: A Comparative Study of Christianisation in Scandinavia.* Occasional Papers in Archaeology 34, Uppsala.

Schroeder, C. 2007. *Monastic Bodies: Discipline and Salvation in Shenoute of Atripe.* Philadelphia, PA: University of Pennsylvania Press.

Scull. C. 1992. 'Before Sutton Hoo: structures of power and society in early East Anglia', in M. Carver (ed.) *The Age of Sutton Hoo: The Seventh Century in North-Western Europe.* Woodbridge: Boydell.

Scull, C. 1993. 'Archaeology, early Anglo-Saxon society and the origins of Anglo-Saxon kingdoms', *Anglo-Saxon Studies in Archaeology and History* 6, 65-82.

Scull, C. 2009. *Early Medieval (Late Fifth-Early Eighth Centuries AD) Cemeteries at Boss Hall and Buttermarket, Ipswich, Suffolk.* Society for Medieval Archaeology Monograph 27. Leeds: Maneys.

Semple, S.J. 1998. 'A fear of the past: the place of the prehistoric burial mound in the ideology of middle and later Anglo-Saxon England', *World Archaeology* 30(1), 109-26.

Semple, S. 2007. 'Defining the OE *hearg*: a preliminary archaeological and topographic examination of *hearg* place names and their hinterlands', *Early Medieval Europe* 15(4), 364-85.

Semple, S. 2010. 'In the open air', in M. Carver (ed.) 2010, 21-48.

Shaw, R. 1990. 'Invention of "African traditional religion"', *Religion* 20, 339-53.

Shaw, T. 1998. *The Burden of the Flesh: Fasting and Sexuality in Early Christianity.* Minneapolis, MN: Fortress.

Sherlock, S. and Simmons, M. 2008. 'A seventh-century royal cemetery at Street House, north-east Yorkshire, England', *Antiquity* 82, http://www.antiquity.ac.uk.ezphost.dur.ac.uk/projgall/sherlock/in dex.html [accessed 15/5/09].

Sims-Williams, P. 1998. 'The uses of writings in early medieval Wales', in H. Pryce (ed.) *Literacy in Medieval Celtic Societies* Cambridge: CUP, 15-39.

Sisam, K. 1953. 'Anglo-Saxon royal genealogies', *Proceedings of the British Academy* 39, 287-346.

Slupecki, L. and Zaroff, R. 1999. 'William of Malmesbury on pagan Slavic oracles', *Studia Mythologica Slavica* 2, 9-20.

Smith, R.A. 1903. 'Anglo-Saxon remains' in *Victoria History of the County of Essex I*, London: Archibald Constable, 315-31.

Bibliography

Speake, G. 1989. *A Saxon Bed Burial on Swallowcliffe Down*. London: Historic Buildings and Monuments Commission for England.

Spriggs, M. 2008. 'Ethnographic parallels and the denial of history', *World Archaeology* 40(4), 538-52.

Spurkland, T, 2001. 'Scandinavian medieval runic inscriptions – an interface between literacy and orality', in J. Higgint, K. Forsyth and D. Parsons (eds) *Roman, Runes and Ogham: Medieval Inscriptions in the Insular World and on the Continent* Donington: Shaun Tyas, 121-8.

Stacey, R.C. 2007. *Dark Speech: Performance of Law in Early Ireland*. Philadelphia: University of Pennsylvania Press.

Staecker, J. 2005. 'The concepts of *imitatio* and *translatio*: perceptions of a Viking-Age past', *Norwegian Archaeological Review* 38, 1-28.

Stocker, D. and Everson, P. 2003. 'The straight and narrow way: fenland causeways and the conversion of the landscape in the Witham Valley, Lincolnshire', in M. Carver (ed.) 2003, 271-88.

Sullivan, R.E. 1966. 'Khan Boris and the conversion of Bulgaria: a case study of the impact of Christianity on a barbarian society', *Studies in Medieval and Renaissance History* 3, 53-139.

Sundqvist, O. 2002. *Freyr's Offspring: Rulers and Religion in Ancient Svea Society*. Acta Universitatis Upsaliensis. Historia Religonum 21. Uppsala.

Tedeschi, C. 1995. 'Osservazioni sulla paleografia delle iscrizioni britanniche paleocristiane (V-VII sec.). Contributo allo studio dell'origine delle scritture insulari', *Scrittura e Civiltà* 19, 67-121.

Tedeschi, C. 2001. 'Some observations on the palaeography of early Christian inscriptions in Britain', in J. Higgit, K. Forsyth and D. Parsons (eds) *Roman, Runes and Ogham: Medieval Inscriptions in the Insular World and on the Continent*. Donington: Shaun Tyas, 16-25.

Teteriatnikov, N. 1992. *The Liturgical Planning of Byzantine Churches in Cappadocia*. London, Rome: Orientalia Christiana Analecta 252.

Thäte, E. 2007. *Monuments and Minds: Monument Re-use in Scandinavia in the Second Half of the First Millennium AD*. Acta Archaeological Lundensia 27, Lund.

Thietmar = D. Warner (ed. & tr.) *Ottonian Germany: the Chronicon of Thietmar of Merseburg*. Manchester: Manchester University Press.

Thomas, C. 1981. *Christianity in Roman Britain to AD 500* London: Batsford.

Tilley, C. 1994. *A Phenomenology of Landscape*. Providence: Berg.

Toop, N. 2005. Dialogues of Power: Early Christian Monumentality around the Northern Irish Sea AD 400-1000. Unpublished PhD dissertation, University of York.

Turner, V. 2003. *The Ritual Process: Structure and Anti-structure.* New York: Aldine de Gruyter.

Tyler, D. 2007. 'Reluctant kings and Christian conversion in seventh-century England', *History* 92, 144-61.

Tylor, E. 1958. *Primitive Culture.* New York: Harper.

Urbanczyk, P. 2003. 'The politics of conversion in North Central Europe', in M. Carver (ed.) 2003, 15-27.

Urbanczyk, P. and Rosik, S. 2007. 'Poland', in N. Berend (ed.) 2007, 264-318.

Van der Meer, F. 1967. *Early Christian Art.* Faber, London: Faber.

Varenius, B. 1995. 'Post-processual archaeology in Sweden 1986-1990', *Current Swedish Archaeology* 3, 121-9.

Vedru, G. 2007. 'Experiencing the landscape', *Estonian Journal of Archaeology* 11, 1, 36-58.

Vita Ansgarii = C.H. Robinson (ed. & tr.) 1921. *Anskar, the Apostle of the North, 801-865.* London: n.p.

Vita Bonifatii = in T.F.X. Noble and T. Head (eds) 1995. *Soldiers of Christ: Saints and Saints' Lives in Late Antiquity and the Early Middle Ages.* University Park: Penn State University Press, 109-40.

Vita Cadoci = *Vita Sancti Cadoci / Life of Saint Cadog*, in A. Wade-Evans (ed. & tr.) 1944. *Vitae Sanctorum Britanniae et Genealogiae.* Cardiff: University of Wales Press, 24-141.

Walker, J. 2010. 'In the hall', in M. Carver et al. (eds) 2010, 83-103.

Watts, D. 1991. *Christians and Pagans in Roman Britain.* London: Routledge.

Webster, L. 1985. 'The grave goods', in J. Hedges and D. Buckley, 'Anglo-Saxon burials and later features excavated at Orsett, Essex 1975', *Medieval Archaeology* 29 9-14 (1-24).

Webster, L. and Backhouse, J. (eds) 1991. *The Golden Age of Anglo-Saxon Art, 966-1066.* London: British Museum.

Wessex Archaeology 2008. 'Amesbury Archer was an Alpine settler say experts', http://www.wessexarch.co.uk/projects/amesbury/press /archer_feb_03_v1.html [accessed 12 September 2010].

Wessman, A. 2010. 'Death, destruction and commemoration: tracing ritual activities in Finnish late Iron Age cemeteries (AD 550-1150)', *ISKOS* 18, Helsinki.

Wharton, A, 1995. *Refiguring the Post Classical City: Dura Europos, Jerash, Jerusalem and Ravenna.* Cambridge: CUP.

Bibliography

Whitehouse, H. and Laidlaw, J. 2004. *Ritual and Memory: Toward a Comparative Anthropology of Religion.* New York: Altamira.

Williams, H. 1997. 'Ancient landscapes and the dead: the reuse of prehistoric and Roman monuments as early Anglo-Saxon burial sites', *Medieval Archaeology* 41: 1-31.

Williams, H. 1999. 'Placing the dead: investigating the location of wealthy barrow burials in seventh century England', in M. Rundkvist (ed.) *Grave Matters: Eight Studies of Burial Data from the First Millennium AD from Crimea, Scandinavia and England.* Oxford: BAR (Int. Ser.) 781, 57-86.

Williams, H. 2006. *Death and Memory in Early Medieval England.* Cambridge: CUP.

Williams, H. 2010. 'Engendered bodies and objects of memory in Final Phase graves', in J. Buckberry and A. Cherryson (eds) *Later Anglo-Saxon Burial c. 650-1100 AD.* Oxford: Oxbow Books, 24-36.

Winterbourne, A. 2004. *When the Norns Have Spoken: Time and Fate in Germanic Paganism.* Madison, NJ: Farleigh Dickinson University Press.

Woolf, A. 1997. 'At home in the long Iron Age: a dialogue between households and individuals in cultural reproduction', in J. Moore and E. Scott (eds) *Invisible People and Processes.* London: Leicester University Press, 68-74.

Yarnold, E. 1978.*The Study of Liturgy.* London: SPCK.

Yorke, B. 1990. *Kings and Kingdoms of Early Anglo-Saxon England.* London: Seaby.

Yorke, B. 2003. 'The adaptation of Anglo-Saxon royal courts to Christianity', in M. Carver (ed.) 2003, 243-57.

Young, B.K. 1999. 'The myth of the pagan cemetery', in C. Karkov, K. Wickham-Crowley and B. Young (eds) *Spaces of the Living and the Dead: An Archaeological Dialogue.* American Early Medieval Studies, no. 3. Oxford: Oxbow Books, 61-85.

Young, B.K. 1977. 'Paganisme, christianisation, et rites funéraires mérovingiens', *Archéologie médiévale* 7, 5-83.

Youngs, S. 1995. 'A penannular brooch from near Calne, Wiltshire', *Wiltshire Archaeological Journal* 8, 127-31.

Zabiela, Z. 2003. 'Late cremation cemeteries of southern Lithuania', *Archaeologia Lituania* 3.

Zachrisson, T. 1994. 'The Odal and its manifestation in the landscape', *Current Swedish Archaeology* 2, 219-38.

Index

Index

Index